SHATTERING THE GLASS OF FEAR AND WALKING FULLY IN FAITH

R. LYNN MOORE

Shattering The Glass Of Fear and Walking Fully In Faith
Copyright © 2022 by R. Lynn Moore

All Rights Reserved

No part of this book may be reproduced or transmitted in any format or by any means without written permission from the author.

ISBN: 9798849904375

DEDICATION

This book is dedicated to my "Daily Moments With God" Facebook Family, my children, and my grandchildren. Thank you for all the love and support that you have given me throughout the years. It is my prayer that this book will be an extension of what God is doing daily in our lives and I pray that it will prove to help countless believers grow from a place of fear and doubt to the place where they are fully walking in faith. It is my prayer that we all continue to pray without ceasing for the Body of Christ and that supernatural miracles will take place in our lives, as well as, the lives of others as a result of each of us walking in faith in Jesus name ... amen.

Chapter 1

Let's Talk About Faith 11

Chapter 2

What Is Your Faith Based On? 18

Chapter 3

Faith Works Through The Process Of Time 29

Chapter 4

What Do You Do While You Wait In Faith? 37

Chapter 5

What Do You Do When Fear Comes To Challenge Your Faith? 43

Chapter 6

What Do You Do When You Feel Weak? Do You Stay In Faith? 49

Chapter 7

What Is Hindering Your Faith? 55

Chapter 8

What It Means To Have Unwavering Faith 61

Chapter 9

A Measure Of Faith 67

Chapter 10

How Faith Comes — 73

Chapter 11

How To Develop Your Faith — 77

Chapter 12

Faith In God Takes Away The Pride Of Self — 83

Chapter 13

Saving Faith — 90

Chapter 14

Sustaining Faith — 96

Chapter 15

What Faith Brings — 102

Chapter 16

What It Means To Have Misplaced Faith — 108

Chapter 17

Limited Faith — 114

Chapter 18

Asking God To Strengthen Your Faith — 119

Chapter 19

Confessing God's Word In Faith — 124

Chapter 20

Building On Your Foundation Of Faith　　　130

Chapter 21

Continuing In Faith　　　140

Chapter 22

Yielding The Fruit Of Your Faith　　　145

Chapter 23

Finishing Faith　　　150

Chapter 24

TALKING ABOUT SCRIPTURE AS IT RELATES TO
YOUR FAITH　　　156

INTRODUCTION

In the world that we are living in right now, fear is prevalent. We are being inundated on a day-to-day basis with things that are meant to cause us to walk in fear. Whether it be situations like Cancer, Covid, Monkeypox, etc. coming against our health or situations coming against our family, our finances, or other parts of our lives, they all have the same agenda, and that is to produce fear in our lives but understand, God wants us to fear NOT! He wants us to be strong in Him and the power of His might. He wants us to walk fully in faith. He wants us to trust Him and to lean not on our own understanding and it is my prayer that this book will help strengthen your faith and shatter the glass of fear that is hindering you in life. I pray that this book will serve as an instrument that you will use to remind yourself that God is with you and He is watching over His Word to perform it in your life.

Sometimes in life we know the Word and all we need is to be reminded of the Word we know. This is not a book that I want you to rush through to read. It is a book that I want you to read, meditate on, answer the questions in, and participate and take the actions steps given to help build your foundation of faith. It is my prayer that as you read through the pages of this book that God will bring to your remembrance His promises to you and if you have never known His promises to you, I pray that He will begin to unveil them to you like never before.

Know that God has not left you. Know that He is always with you. Know that there is nothing that the heavenly Father will withhold from you that is in alignment with His Word and will for your life.

As you read through the pages of this book, I want you to ask yourself the following questions:

- What is holding you back?
- What is it that you see God doing for others that you are sitting back hoping and wishing He would do for you?
- What has you self-contained in life where you feel as though you are locked up in a place where you can't get past the fear of failure in your life?
- What is it that is keeping you locked behind the glass of fear where you only have a limited view of God and a limited amount of faith in God?

I am praying that this book helps you to shatter the glass of fear in your life that is holding you back, restraining you, and containing your faith and I pray that it helps you to move forward to the point that you can walk fully in faith with God. Keep in mind as you read this book that the word shatter means to impair, to weaken, and to destroy. I pray that fear will no longer have the power to hinder you in your walk of faith with God in Jesus name ... amen.

R. Lynn Moore, Author

Chapter 1
LET'S TALK ABOUT FAITH

The Bible says that without faith it is impossible to please God. In life different things bring different people pleasure but the Bible says that it is our faith in God that pleases Him and our greatest desire in life should always be to bring pleasure to God. The Bible also says that faith is the substance of things hoped for and the evidence of things not seen. When you have substance, it is something you can hold onto and when you have evidence, you can prove that something is real. Your faith is your substance and it is also your evidence. As you hold on to your faith and as God honors His Word in your life by bringing the objective of your faith to pass, it in turn proves that He is real. What we must always remember is the things we are asking God for in faith should always be in alignment with His written Word.

As we think about breaking the glass of fear in our lives, we have to understand that the only way to conquer fear is by walking fully in faith. We have to stand on faith, walk in faith, and live by faith. Your faith needs to be steadfast and immovable undoubtedly because fear will come. Your faith should not be something that comes and goes. True faith does not waver and it does not fluctuate like the stock market or blow around with the winds of life. True faith has to be constant, unshakeable, unmovable, and undeniable. Understand, if you are fluctuating in faith, you have an element of doubt working within you and you are questioning within yourself whether or not you can truly trust and believe that God will move on your behalf.

Faith in God has to be rooted and grounded in your trust in God and your love for God. If there are no roots to your faith, then your faith will fail and you will continue to dwell behind the glass of fear. Instead of being rooted and grounded in God and His promises, you will become anxious, shakeable, and fearful when it comes to trusting and believing God. Fear should not be your residence in life. It should not be the place where you dwell. You should not be living your life constantly looking out of the window or glass of fear wondering if God will do what He said He would do if you step out in faith.

In order for us to walk in faith with God, we must first understand what Godly faith is. You can't walk out on what you do not know. Trying to walk out on what you do not know is like living in a house with no foundation or like having sinkholes all around your house that could collapse on you at any moment in time. Our faith in God is our confidence and our trust in God's ability to do what He has said He would do. Faith is about trusting God to honor His Word to us and to also trusting Him to perfect His Word in us and through us. Do you trust God? Do you trust Him to do what He said He would do for you, in you, and through you? Do you believe that He will honor His Word in your life?

AS WE BEGIN TO SHATTER THE GLASS OF FEAR, <u>WE MUST UNDERSTAND</u> THAT ...

✳ We must stand firm in our faith. When something is firm, it tends to be resistant when external pressure is applied. It is resilient and it is in a secure place. When you are firm, you don't fluctuate and you don't move.

> *Ephesians 6:13*
> *Wherefore take unto you the whole armour of God, that ye may be able to withstand in the evil day, and having done all, to stand.*

✳ We must walk by faith. Walking requires that you move (unlike standing firm). When you walk by faith, your movement is synchronized and in alignment with God's Word and will for your life.

> *2 Corinthians 5:7*
> *For we walk by faith, not by sight:*

✻ We must live by faith. Living by faith says that you have a lifestyle of faith. Your lifestyle is how you style your life. A life that is styled by faith is a life that is adorned by God. When something is adorned, it is enhanced and it is made beautiful. So understand, a faith filled life is enhanced and made more beautiful as God honors His promises in accordance to His Word. When we live by faith, we wait in hope and expectation for God to honor His Word in our lives.

> *Galatians 2:20*
> *I am crucified with Christ: nevertheless I live; yet not I, but Christ liveth in me: and the life which I now live in the flesh I live by the faith of the Son of God, who loved me, and gave Himself for me.*

AS YOU SHATTER THE GLASS OF FEAR IN YOUR LIFE, ASK YOURSELF ...

Are you standing, walking, and living by faith? Faith requires us to stand on God's Word, to walk according to His Word, and to live our lives based on His Word. When something is based on something else, it is founded, established, and focused on whatever it is based upon.

ACTION STEP: Examine yourself! Think about 3 examples that reflect how you are "standing" in faith, "walking" in faith, and "living" by faith. The Bible says we are to examine ourselves and to prove our own-selves.

We have to know the importance of self-examination and we need to make sure that we are taking an optimistic approach to examining ourselves and not a pessimistic one. When you look at life and the situations in your life from an optimistic view, your thoughts begin to focus more on your positives and minimizes the negatives in your life. Whereas, a pessimistic view of your life, will always focus in on the negatives and overestimate and highlight the risks that will hinder you from fully walking in faith. Overestimating and highlighting the risks in your life will always keep you living behind the glass of fear. Whereas, focusing in on what is positive and knowing that God can do all things for you, in you, and through you, will help you to break the glass of fear so that you can move forward with God.

II Corinthians 13:5
Examine yourselves, whether ye be in the faith; prove your ownselves. Know ye not your ownselves, how that Jesus Christ is in you, except ye be reprobates?

Whether you write it here, in a journal, or on another piece of paper, take time to write down the answers to the following:

1) One way you are standing in faith (Standing in faith means that after you have prayed, you are being still and trusting God to do what you are asking Him to do.)

   _____
   _____
   _____
   _____

2) One way you are walking in faith (Walking in faith means that you have prayed and you are doing something in preparation for God to do what you are asking Him to do.)

   _____
   _____
   _____
   _____

3) One way you are living by faith (Living by faith means you have prayed and you are doing all that God has told you to do and you are waiting in hope and expectation for God to do what only He can do.)

   _____
   _____
   _____
   _____

CONFESSION

Father today is a new day and today I will shatter the glass of fear that has been holding me captive in life. Father I know today that my faith is the substance of the things I am hoping for and the evidence of the things I have yet to see. Father I commit to standing firm in faith, walking by faith, and living my life by faith. I commit to holding on to my faith as I break the glass of fear in my life. Father today as I shatter fear, I bind up and I cast down everything in my life that is exalting itself against the knowledge I have of who You are and what you have said You will do in me, for me, and through me. Father today I choose to please You and I know that it is impossible to please you without faith. So today, I choose to stand in faith, I choose to walk by faith, and I choose to live a lifestyle of faith. Father today I choose to stay in faith in Jesus name ... amen.

STOP

TAKE TIME TO MEDITATE ON WHAT YOU HAVE READ, THE QUESTIONS YOU HAVE ANSWERED, AND THE STEPS YOU HAVE TAKEN BEFORE PROCEEDING TO THE NEXT CHAPTER OF THIS BOOK.

Chapter 2
WHAT IS YOUR FAITH BASED ON?

As we look at shattering the glass of fear and walking fully in faith, you need to ask yourself what is the basis of your faith? In other words, what is the foundation for what you say you believe? We can have faith in anything. We can have faith in God, faith in people, faith in things, and we can even have faith in fear.

Faith is believing in someone or something without having sense realm evidence. Sense realm evidence is evidence based on your five senses. Things you can see, hear, smell, touch, and taste. When we walk in spiritual faith in God, we just have to believe that God is who He said He is and that He can do what He said He could and would do. We have to believe regardless of what our five senses are telling us. Our sense realm cannot be what we base our faith on because with the sense realm comes a myriad of feelings and emotions which are directly connected to our flesh and we know that our flesh and our Spirit are contrary one to the other. Not to mention, our flesh is the birthing ground of sin. When you look at the fact that our flesh is the birthing ground of sin, you begin to understand that you cannot fully walk in faith if you are going to be moved or led by what you are seeing with your eyes or feeling in your flesh.

> *Galatians 5:17-23*
> *For the flesh lusteth against the Spirit, and the Spirit against the flesh: and these are contrary the one to the other: so that ye cannot do the things that ye would. But if ye be led of the Spirit, ye are not under the law. Now the works of the flesh are manifest, which are these;*
> *Adultery, fornication, uncleanness, lasciviousness, Idolatry, witchcraft, hatred, variance, emulations, wrath, strife, seditions, heresies, envyings, murders, drunkenness, revellings, and such like: of the which I tell you before, as I have also told you in time past, that they which do such things shall not inherit the kingdom of God.*
>
> *But the fruit of the Spirit is love, joy, peace, longsuffering, gentleness, goodness, faith, meekness, temperance: against such there is no law.*

Our faith in God has to be based on our trust and belief in God and His Word. We can't see God the way we see other people with our eyes in the natural realm; we can't hear Him the way we hear other voices and sounds in the earth; nor can we touch Him in this natural realm with our hands the way we are able to touch other things around us but that does not mean that He does not exist. It only means that we have to see Him, hear Him, and touch Him in a spiritual way because He is a spiritual being and that is in itself requires us to relate to Him differently.

We have to see God and live for God spiritually and not naturally. That is why our relationship with God has to be based on Spirit and truth because that is who and what He is. He is a Spirit and He is the Truth. We have to stop trying to live by our fleshly senses when it comes to relating to God. As long as we live by the flesh, we will never be able to truly live by the Spirit and be in constant communion with God. Remember, we cannot let our sense realm understanding override our spiritual realm understanding of who God is and how He relates to us when we walk in faith.

The Bible talks to us about walking in faith and not by sight in 2 Corinthians 5:17. When we try to walk by sight instead of by faith, we see God differently. In some cases it causes us to see Him behind that glass of fear because we don't know how to get past that glass into the place of faith where He wants us to be where we can see His attributes clearly, hear His voice distinctly, and feel His love undoubtedly.

As you think about your five senses, think about what God said in His Word. When it relates to hearing, God told us that faith comes by hearing. He wants us to hear the voice of His command. He said that His sheep hear His voice and the voice of a stranger they will not follow. That is not necessarily an audible voice. We have to know that God is always speaking to us through His Word and relaying to us through His Holy Spirit. God has many ways of getting His message to us but every message from God must be received in our Spirit and every message from God will always be in alignment with His Word and His will. We have to be sure that we are discerning the voices we are adhering and aligning our lives too. The voice of God is clear and distinct in that it does not stray from His written Word and it will never lead you into a place of sin. So if the voice that you are hearing in your Spirit is telling you to do something that is outside of what you know is the will and the Word of God, you can rest assured you are not hearing the voice of God.

As you think about the sense of sight, you understand it is your ability to see. We know that no one has ever physically seen God but Jesus who was sent from God. However, we can see God and His attributes at work at all times through His creation. We see Him through other people when we see those people displaying His characteristics. It is like when you have children. Have you ever had someone to say that they can see you in your children or your mom or dad in you? That is how we should want others to see us as it relates to God. That is how we should be seeing other Christians as it relates to God. We should be seeing the attributes of God and the fruit of His Spirit being reflected in the lives of others and others should see the same in us. The most prevalent of those attributes that should be seen by us and through us should be the love of God.

Love is not something tangible that we can feel and hold with our hands but it is something tangible that we have to hold onto emotionally. When we hold on to the love of God, it gives us hope. Our love for God and His love for us is what gives us hope. When our hope is in God, we are confident in His ability, we trust Him, and we expect Him to move in our lives. Love is a divine connection with another person or thing and it is in essence an anchor. Understand, the purpose of an anchor is to keep things in place and to help control movement. As we stay anchored to God, it stabilizes us and keeps us from being moved to and fro in our faith but we can't let our anchor keep us from moving forward in faith. Understand, even though you are anchored to God by His love, fear can still immobilize you and cause you to be stuck to the point that you are not walking fully in faith. We have to make sure that the anchors on our lives are used appropriately and we have to make sure that we are never anchored in a place of fear to the point that we are afraid to move forward with God.

We can't regulate God to the natural realm and expect to see Him the same way we see other people, places, and things. There is nothing natural about God. When something is natural, it is ordinary and it is produced by nature. We have to always remember the fact that nature was produced by God and not God by nature. God is a spiritual being and we can only see and understand Him with our spiritual senses. Walking in faith is not natural, so you can't truly walk in faith unless you are looking at life through the spiritual lens of who God is and what He has said. You have to also know and believe that all things are possible in and with God.

Ask yourself today whether or not your faith is based on fact or fiction? A fact is something that is known and it has been proven to be true. Whereas, fiction opposes facts. Fiction is a statement or belief that is false and yet in some instances it is held to be true because it is convenient or practical to do so. We have to remember, God's Word is true. It is filled with facts about what was, what is, and what will come. It is not based on our imagination. It is based on what God has said and we have to know, trust, and believe that God is true and what He has said is the truth.

As I opened up this chapter I asked the question, what is the basis of your faith? Do you understand what it means to have something based on something else? When you have a base, it means you have a firm foundation and a point of reference from which something can grow. What is the firm foundation for your faith and from what reference point is your faith growing? Your faith has to be based on the Word of God because with the Word comes spiritual growth and maturity.

AS WE BEGIN TO SHATTER THE GLASS OF FEAR, <u>WE MUST UNDERSTAND</u> THAT …

✽ The Word of God has to be the foundation for your faith. When we think about the foundation of all things, we have to go back to the beginning. We have to go back to when God created the heaven and the earth. He created everything in the beginning, even our faith.

> *John 1:1-3*
> *In the beginning was the Word. And the Word was with God and the Word was God; All things were made through him and without him nothing came to be.*

✷ Faith is not based on sense realm evidence. When we think about faith, we must understand that faith will never coincide with our human intellect. Spiritual faith will never come into agreement with natural sight. Our spiritual realm understanding always has to override what we see and understand in the natural realm.

> *2 Corinthians 4:18*
> *While we look not at the things which are seen, but at the things which are not seen: for the things which are seen are temporal; but the things which are not seen are eternal. The love of God is an anchor for our soul.*

✷ We have to be anchored to God but we should never be anchored to fear. Our faith and love for God and His love for us is something that is tangible that we can hold onto and it gives us hope. We have to always remember that our anchor of hope is to God and not to people, places, or things. God's anchor is meant to hold us in line with His Word and His will but not to keep us in a place of fear. We have to be conscious of who and what we anchor ourselves to. Sometimes we anchor ourselves to people, places, and things. When we anchor ourselves to people, places, and things, we run the risk of not just being anchored, we may even become attached to them. That is where soul-ties come in. When we attach ourselves to the wrong things that appeal to our mind, our will, and our emotions, we create soul-ties. When we create soul-ties, we can become attached to the point that we become afraid to let go and move forward with God in faith and we end up stuck behind a glass of fear and possibly disobedience.

> *Hebrews 6:19*
> *Which hope we have as an anchor of the soul, both sure and stedfast, and which entereth into that within the veil;*

AS YOU SHATTER THE GLASS OF FEAR IN YOUR LIFE, ASK YOURSELF ...

Is your faith rooted and grounded in the Word of God? When something is rooted, it is fixed in a particular position. It is unable to be moved. When something is grounded, it is stable and it is secure. The thing about grounded wires is that they are buried as a safety measure to help prevent a house fire or electrical shock. The grounded wires act as a shock absorber and redirects electrical charges to where they need to go. That is what the Word of God is meant to do for us. When we come against trials and temptation in our lives, the Word of God should rise up within us and help us to redirect our thoughts and our actions and keep us in a place of safety in and with God. We have to stay rooted and we have to stay grounded so that the fiery darts of the enemy will have no affect on our lives.

ACTION STEP: Take a moment and think about what you are asking God for. Now check and make sure that your requests to God are in line with the Word of God. Make sure what you say you are believing God for is based on the Word of God and not a fleshly desire. Check the thoughts and intents of your heart as you make your requests known to God.

Also, as you make your requests known to God, make sure you are asking God from a position of faith and not a position of fear. When you ask God for something from a position of faith, there is confidence and expectation for Him to honor His Word in your life. When you ask God for something from a position of fear, you are asking God, hoping that He will move but there is still an element of doubt in your heart as to whether He will move on your behalf or not. You have to remember that you are shattering the glass of fear and committing to walking fully in faith.

> *Hebrews 4:12*
> *For the word of God [is] quick, and powerful, and sharper than any twoedged sword, piercing even to the dividing asunder of soul and spirit, and of the joints and marrow, and [is] a discerner of the thoughts and intents of the heart.*

Whether you write it here, in a journal, or on another piece of paper, take time to write down the answers to the following:

1) What are 2 things that you have been asking God to "give you or do for you in life"?

   _____
   _____
   _____
   _____
   _____
   _____

2) Write out 2 scriptures that relate to what you are asking God for.

   _____
   _____
   _____
   _____
   _____
   _____

CONFESSION

Father You are the basis of my faith. My life is situated on You and Your Word. Father I will stay anchored to You. I will not allow myself to let people, places, or things take the place that You should be occupying in my life. Father thank You for showing me what it means to walk by faith and not by sight. Thank You for helping me to use my spiritual senses when it comes to living my life. Father my faith is in You. My hope is in You. My confidence is in You. I trust You Father to help me to shatter the glass of fear that is trying to cause me to be in bondage in life. Help me Father to walk fully in faith in Jesus name ... amen.

STOP
TAKE TIME TO MEDITATE ON WHAT YOU HAVE READ, THE QUESTIONS YOU HAVE ANSWERED, AND THE STEPS YOU HAVE TAKEN BEFORE PROCEEDING TO THE NEXT CHAPTER OF THIS BOOK.

Chapter 3
FAITH WORKS THROUGH THE PROCESS OF TIME

Do you have a right now faith? The kind of faith that wants things to happen right now and if it doesn't happen right now, the kind of faith that causes you to become worried and discontent? Are you stuck behind a glass of fear because you are not understanding God's process of time? Are you becoming impatient and doubting if God will honor His Word in your life because nothing is working out how and when you thought it would? If that is you, know that we have all been there. Know that we have all been at that place where we ask God why and when. We tend to ask God why is this happening and when will this change. What we have to understand is faith is not always fast, sometimes the manifestation of what we are asking God for in faith takes time to show up in our lives.

In this world that we live in today, it is hard to process the fact that sometimes, some things, take time. We live in what I like to call a microwave society. A society where no one likes to wait for anything. We go to fast food restaurants and we get upset if it takes too long to get our food. We get online and get upset if it takes too long to load a page on the internet. We get in our cars and get frustrated when we have to sit in traffic because it is taking too long to get to our destination. We even get upset if we try to call someone and it takes too long for the call to connect or for them to answer. We want and even expect everything in our lives to happen quickly or should I say immediately. That is how we are with God and with our faith. We want to walk in a "right now" faith where we tell God or expect God to do it right now. There will be times when God will move immediately for us but we have to also understand that there may be times when we have to wait on God to do what only He can do and when we have to wait, we need to wait with the right mindset and the right heart attitude. We need to wait on God and we can't let the glass of fear keep us from stepping out on faith and asking God to honor His Word of faith in our lives nor can we allow it to cause us to be in fear because of the process of time.

Over and over in God's Word He encourages us to wait on Him and He tells us how He wants us to wait. God has told us to patiently wait on Him, to be obedient while we wait on Him, and to have courage while we wait on Him. God doesn't want us to be anxious for anything. He wants us to have faith and He wants us to know that if we wait on Him, He will honor His Word in our lives.

Understand, it is our human nature to want things right now because of this fast paced society we are living in but we have to learn how to listen to God and follow His instructions and know that He will honor His Word in our lives even if the results of our faith takes time to manifest. We always have to remember that times and seasons are in God's hand. So that means the time and the season for our breakthroughs in life have already been set in place by God and He knows when that time is. Not only does He know when that time is, He has already prepared His blessings to come forth at that particular time. We just have to trust His timing.

AS WE BEGIN TO SHATTER THE GLASS OF FEAR, <u>WE MUST UNDERSTAND</u> THAT ...

* God wants us to wait. Waiting on God means you are in a place of expectation and readiness. It means you cease from moving and trying to do things on your own. It means you stay in place until the person or the things that you are waiting on catches up with you.

> *Psalm 37:34*
> *Wait on the Lord, and keep His way, and He shall exalt thee to inherit the land: when the wicked are cut off, thou shalt see it.*

* God wants us to be patient as we wait on Him to fulfill His promises. He doesn't want us to be complacent and

careless as we wait. He wants us to wait in faith, with hope and expectation for Him to do what He said He would do.

> *Hebrews 6:12-15*
> *That ye be not slothful, but followers of them who through faith and patience inherit the promises. For when God made promise to Abraham, because He could swear by no greater, He sware by Himself, Saying, Surely blessing I will bless thee, and multiplying I will multiply thee. And so, after he had patiently endured, he obtained the promise.*

* God wants us to be still while we wait. He wants at peace. He wants us free from worry and free from fear. He does not want our faith in Him to fluctuate to where we believe Him at times and doubt Him at other times. When you are still, you are not moving. You are not fluctuating back and forth. You have a calmness even when turmoil is going on all around you.

> *Psalm 46:10*
> *Be still, and know that I am God: I will be exalted among the heathen, I will be exalted in the earth.*

✷ God doesn't want us to be anxious. When you are anxious, you are uneasy and apprehensive. Your level of fear may be intensified based on how you are interpreting the possible outcome of your situation. Anxiety can also cause you to jump to conclusions instead of staying in a place of faith.

> *Philippians 4:6*
> *Be careful for nothing; but in everything by prayer and supplication with thanksgiving let your requests be made known unto God.*

AS YOU SHATTER THE GLASS OF FEAR IN YOUR LIFE, ASK YOURSELF ...

Are you content with waiting on God to fulfill His promises in your life or do you have an "I want it right now" mentality? Are you exhibiting patience in your process of waiting? Are you jumping to conclusions about your outcome because of the time that it is taking to receive an answer from God?

ACTION STEP: Thinking about what waiting on God means to you, look up and write down the meaning of the words wait, patient, still, and rest.

> *Psalm 37:7a*
> *Rest in the Lord, and wait patiently for Him:*

Whether you write it here, in a journal, or on another piece of paper, take time to write down the answers to the following:

1) Define "Wait"

_____
_____
_____
_____

2) Define "Patient"

_____
_____
_____
_____

3) Define "Still"

_____
_____
_____

Shattering The Glass Of Fear   Walking Fully In Faith

4) Define "Rest"

_____
_____
_____
_____

CONFESSION

Father I know that faith can sometimes take time and I commit right now to waiting on You. Father Your Word says for me to be still and to know that you are God. So today that is what I will do. I will not be caught up on how long the process is taking, instead I will be patient and I will be still. I will not let anxiety consume me and keep me behind the glass of fear. I will continue to step out on faith, stand in faith, and walk fully in faith because my hope, my trust, and my expectation are all in You. Father, You are God and you have called me out of darkness into Your marvelous light. Thank You Father for never leaving me nor forsaking me. Thank You for doing in me and for me what only You can do in Jesus name ... Amen.

STOP

TAKE TIME TO MEDITATE ON WHAT YOU HAVE READ, THE QUESTIONS YOU HAVE ANSWERED, AND THE STEPS YOU HAVE TAKEN BEFORE PROCEEDING TO THE NEXT CHAPTER OF THIS BOOK.

Chapter 4
WHAT DO YOU DO WHILE YOU WAIT IN FAITH?

What are you going to do while you wait? That's the big question. A lot of times we just don't know what to do. We get antsy, we get fearful, and sometimes we even give up while we are waiting. We have to remember what God said. He said through faith and patience we shall obtain the promise. When you are antsy, you are restless, fidgety, impatient, and eager. All of those are obvious emotions that arise when the thing you are in faith for appears to be delayed. Eagerness says you want to have something very much but you can't let your eagerness override your patience as you wait on God.

How you wait and what you do as you wait are two important factors. Are you waiting patiently in expectation or are you impatiently waiting and wishing for God to move quickly in your life? Don't allow your impatience to cause an even greater delay because you are outside of God's Word, His will, and His timing.

One of the most important things we must do while we wait on God is to seek Him. You have to stay in a place where you are constantly seeking God and expecting Him to move in your life. You cannot stay behind a glass of fear when it comes to seeking God. You have to be in a place where you can see Him clearly and follow Him faithfully. God said in His Word that if we seek Him, we shall find Him. Think about what it means to seek someone or something. It means to look for something intensely and intentionally. Now think about the feeling you have when you find what you have been looking for. When you find something that has been lost or even finding something for the first time, you get excited and sometimes even overwhelmed with joy, peace, and confidence. That is the same feeling you should feel as you seek God and find Him moving in your life. You should be filled with awe and you should be filled with excitement.

As you wait on God, you should also be filled with hope and expectation. If you are constantly walking in fear, you can't walk in hope. Fear and hope oppose one another. Fear brings with it anxiety and hope brings with it expectation. Again, we must shatter the glass of fear so that we can fully walk in faith and with faith comes hope and expectation for God to do what He said He would do.

AS WE BEGIN TO SHATTER THE GLASS OF FEAR, <u>WE MUST UNDERSTAND</u> THAT ...

* We must wait in expectation. When you wait in expectation, it affects how you think. It causes you to look forward to something and it causes you to walk in anticipation. God wants us to be in constant anticipation and expectation as we wait on Him to fulfill His promises in our lives.

> *Psalms 62:5*
> *My soul, wait thou only upon God; for my expectation is from Him.*

* We must seek God while we wait and in order to find God, we must seek Him with our whole heart. When you seek something you try to locate it or discover it. You move towards it. You earnestly attempt to get something on purpose. God wants us to make the effort so that we can find Him on purpose. He wants us to look for Him in His Word, He wants us to seek Him through prayer, and He wants us to seek to know His will in every situation concerning our lives.

> *Lamentations 3:25*
> *The LORD [is] good unto them that wait for Him, to the soul [that] seeketh Him.*

> *Jeremiah 29:13*
> *And ye shall seek me, and find me, when ye shall search for me with all your heart.*

AS YOU SHATTER THE GLASS OF FEAR IN YOUR LIFE, ASK YOURSELF ...

Are you truly seeking God with with your whole heart? Do you understand that God is looking down from heaven to see if you are seeking Him according to Psalms 14:2?

> *Psalms 14:2*
> *The LORD looked down from heaven upon the children of men, to see if there were any that did understand, and seek God.*

ACTION STEP: Check Your Heart! When God says to seek Him with your whole heart, that means to seek Him wholeheartedly. That means your heart is not divided. It means your heart is at peace and on one accord with Him. God wants us to draw near to Him, He wants us to seek Him, and He wants us to find Him. Take a moment to write down a scripture about drawing near to God, seeking God, and finding God. Meditate on those scriptures for the next 3 days.

> *Psalm 119:10*
> *With my whole heart have I sought thee: O let me not wander from thy commandments.*

Whether you write it here, in a journal, or on another piece of paper, take time to write down the answers to the following:

1) Write down a scripture about drawing near to God.

   _____
   _____
   _____
   _____

2) Write down a scripture about seeking God.

   _____
   _____
   _____
   _____

3) Write down a scripture about finding God.

   _____
   _____
   _____
   _____

CONFESSION

Today Father I commit myself to You. I commit my words to You, my actions to You, and my heart to You. Father I want my life to be on one accord with You. Your Word says if I seek You, I shall find You. Thank You Father for always being with me and for always showing me the way You would have me to go. Thank You for teaching me how to shatter the glass of fear in my life and how to draw close to You. Today I commit to seeking You with my whole heart while I wait on You to fulfill Your promises in my life in Jesus name ... amen.

STOP

TAKE TIME TO MEDITATE ON WHAT YOU HAVE READ, THE QUESTIONS YOU HAVE ANSWERED, AND THE STEPS YOU HAVE TAKEN BEFORE PROCEEDING TO THE NEXT CHAPTER OF THIS BOOK.

Chapter 5
WHAT DO YOU DO WHEN FEAR COMES TO CHALLENGE YOUR FAITH?

What do you do when you are faced with fear? When the glass of fear comes face-to-face with you. There may be times in your life where you see yourself and feel yourself walking in fear. What do you do? One of the biggest challenges that we have to overcome in life is when fear comes to challenge our faith.

It is easy to walk in faith when everything seems to be going your way. When situations are in perfect alignment with "your" expectation. What happens when things get out of line? What happens when you hit a roadblock and have to reroute "your thinking" and you don't know which way to go? Do you at that point allow the unknown to keep you from believing that God can and will make a way for you or do you press on and press through whatever it is that is hindering you so that you can experience God's best for your life?

Fear can cause our faith to freeze. When your faith freezes, it becomes motionless. It stops. God wants our faith to have movement. He wants us to have faith that will move mountains. Faith that will bring about change. Faith that believes and faith that receives the promises of God and we can't let the glass of fear stop us from trusting, hoping, believing, and receiving the promises of God.

We have to know how to bind up and cast down fear. We have to make up in our mind that fear has no place in us because fear counteracts our faith. When we are fearful or overwhelmed by fear, we fail to put our hope and trust in God. Trust and hope make up the foundation of faith. You have to believe in God's truth, His ability, His strength, and His power to do whatever needs to be done. If you don't believe in God's truth, ability, strength, and power, you can never receive what you are asking God for by faith. We must believe in who God is and what God is able to do in order to receive His supernatural blessings in our lives. Our faith in God has to conquer all the fear we come up against in this world.

AS WE BEGIN TO SHATTER THE GLASS OF FEAR, <u>WE MUST UNDERSTAND</u> THAT ...

* Fear is meant to trap or snare you. When something traps you or snares you, it lures you, entangles you, and confines you. That is what fear does. He keeps you in a place where you are not able to move freely with God.

Understand, a trap is set in an effort to catch you off-guard.

> *Proverbs 29:25*
> *The fear of man bringeth a snare: but whoso putteth his trust in the LORD shall be safe.*

* When you are afraid, you have to put your trust in God. Understand, fear leaves you feeling frail. When you are frail, you are not strong and you are easily broken. When your trust is in God, you know that He is your strength and you cannot be broken.

> *Psalms 56:3-4*
> *What time I am afraid, I will trust in thee. In God I will praise His Word, in God I have put my trust; I will not fear what flesh can do unto me.*

* Seeking God delivers you from the bondage of fear because it causes you to shift your focus and it keeps your mind stayed on God.

> *Psalms 34:4*
> *I sought the LORD, and He heard me, and delivered me from all my fears.*

AS YOU SHATTER THE GLASS OF FEAR IN YOUR LIFE, ASK YOURSELF ...

Have you bound up and cast down every thought in your mind that is exalting itself against the knowledge you have of who God is and what He will do for you?

ACTION STEP: Counteract every word that is coming up in your mind that is causing you to be in fear with a Word that encourages you to walk in faith. Take a look at the following statements and write down one word or a scripture that counteracts each statement. Always let God's Word override the enemy's words in your life.

> *Proverbs 12:25*
> *Heaviness in the heart of man maketh it stoop:*
> *but a good word maketh it glad.*

Whether you write it here, in a journal, or on another piece of paper, take time to write down the answers to the following:

1) Instead of saying I am afraid, what should you say?

_____
_____
_____
_____

2) Instead of saying I can't do it, what should you say?

_____
_____
_____
_____

3) Instead of saying I don't have enough, what should you say?

_____
_____
_____
_____

4) Instead of saying I am lost, what should you say?

_____
_____
_____
_____

CONFESSION

Father I will not be afraid and therefore I will not dwell behind the glass of fear. Today I speak life over my life and I will not allow fear to trap me or to snare me unexpectedly. If I hit a roadblock in life today, I will press forward in and with you. I will not speak negatively about my situation and every thought that rises up against the knowledge of what You have said about me I will bind up and cast down. Father I cast all of my care upon you because I know that You care for me. My faith will not be frozen by fear. I will say what you say about me and the situations that concern my life. I will seek you wholeheartedly and I will wait in hope and expectation for You to do what only You can do in me and for me in Jesus name ... Amen.

STOP
TAKE TIME TO MEDITATE ON WHAT YOU HAVE READ, THE QUESTIONS YOU HAVE ANSWERED, AND THE STEPS YOU HAVE TAKEN BEFORE PROCEEDING TO THE NEXT CHAPTER OF THIS BOOK.

Chapter 6
WHAT DO YOU DO WHEN YOU FEEL WEAK? DO YOU STAY IN FAITH?

Sometimes we feel weak and we don't feel as though we can get past the glass of fear, nevertheless, shatter it. When you feel weak you feel as though you don't have the strength or the energy to deal with things in your life. When you are at that point you have to know how to cast your cares on God because He cares for you. God never called us to walk this walk alone. He has always told us that He is with us. He even said He will never leave us nor forsake us. That is why in our weakness, He is strong. We have to understand that it is not in our strength that we are able to accomplish anything; it is only in God's power, ability, and strength that we are able to live, breathe, and have our being.

We have to stop trying to walk this walk alone. We have to stop trying to figure life out on our own. We have to learn how to truly lean on and rest in God. The thing about leaning on something or someone is that you have a support system. When something or someone supports you, they bear all of the weight or part of the weight in order to hold you up. God and His Word are our support system. His Word supports us, encourages us, and it tells us how to cast our cares on Him and how to lean on and trust in Him. When we understand these things we know that even in our weakness God is strong and our faith should be in what God can do for us and not what we can do for ourselves.

AS WE BEGIN TO SHATTER THE GLASS OF FEAR, WE MUST UNDERSTAND THAT ...

* God wants us to trust Him and to lean on Him. When you trust someone, you have confidence in them. Confidence says that you believe in their ability. God wants us to believe in His ability to take care of us. Leaning on someone or something, also means you depend on it or them for support and you are not limited to your own strength or your own ability to do something or to make something happen.

> *Proverbs 3:5-6*
> *Trust in the Lord with all thine heart; and lean not unto thine own understanding. In all thy ways acknowledge Him, and He shall direct thy paths.*

✳ God wants us to cast the weight of our worry on Him. Weight is a force of gravity that is heavy. God does not want us weighted down with the heaviness of worry in our lives. Heaviness is a state of mind that brings with it grief, distress, agony, and hopelessness; none of which God wants for us.

> *1 Peter 5:7*
> *Casting all your care upon Him; for He careth for you.*

✳ We have to remember, God's grace is sufficient for us and His strength is made perfect in our weakness. When something is sufficient, it is more than enough. When something is made perfect, it is made without flaws. So there is nothing imperfect about the strength of of God and the grace of God is immeasurable.

> *2 Corinthians 12:9-10*
> *And He said unto me, My grace is sufficient for thee: for My strength is made perfect in weakness. Most gladly therefore will I rather glory in my infirmities, that the power of Christ may rest upon me. Therefore I take pleasure in infirmities, in reproaches, in necessities, in persecutions, in distresses for Christ's sake: for when I am weak, then am I strong.*

AS YOU SHATTER THE GLASS OF FEAR IN YOUR LIFE, ASK YOURSELF ...

Are you turning to the Word of God to encourage and strengthen yourself when you feel weak or are you looking to get strength from other people, places, or things?

ACTION STEP: Write down a list of at least 5 scriptures that talk about God strengthening you. God wants us to be strong in Him. He wants us to remember, greater is He that is in us than anything coming against us in this world. That means that there is nothing in this world that is stronger than God and His power in the earth and we have to remember that it is His strength that is at work in us.

> *Psalm 18:1-2*
> *I will love thee, O Lord, my strength. The Lord is my rock, and my fortress, and my deliverer; my God, my strength, in whom I will trust; my buckler, and the horn of my salvation, and my high tower.*

Whether you write it here, in a journal, or on another piece of paper, take time to write down the answers .

1) _____
   _____
   _____
   _____

2) _____
_____
_____
_____

3) _____
_____
_____
_____

4) _____
_____
_____
_____

5) _____
_____
_____
_____

CONFESSION

Father today as I shatter the glass of fear in my life, I commit to standing strong in You. I know that You are my Rock, my Fortress, my Deliverer, and my Strength. There is nothing that You are not. Father, I declare and decree today that my strength shall not fail. I shall stay in faith. I will draw from the well of Your Word within me. In the times when I feel weak I will always remember and confess the fact that it is You and Your strength that is at work in me and Your strength is made perfect in my weakness. Father my hope is in You and I know that Your Holy Spirit is at work in me and greater are You in me than anything that can ever come up against me in this world in Jesus name ... amen.

STOP

TAKE TIME TO MEDITATE ON WHAT YOU HAVE READ, THE QUESTIONS YOU HAVE ANSWERED, AND THE STEPS YOU HAVE TAKEN BEFORE PROCEEDING TO THE NEXT CHAPTER OF THIS BOOK.

Chapter 7
WHAT IS HINDERING YOUR FAITH?

Walking in faith is not an easy thing to do because faith has to believe in the unseen. We as people tend to believe in what we can see. We see a chair and we believe the chair can hold us so we have faith in the chair's ability to hold us up and yet we struggle with believing that God, who created all things, can and will hold us up too. We tend to forget that it was God who created the chair and gave it the ability to hold our weight. Biblical faith is not belief in what we can see, it is belief in God whom we cannot see. It is belief in God's ability. In other words, it is belief in the Creator and not just the things He creates.

We have to learn that when we see things through our natural eyes we are not to accept them as final and true if they go against what God has said. We have to see what God sees and say what God has said. He said that our faith can move mountains. He said that He is with us and He said that He would watch over us. Understand, faith begins by taking God at His Word and believing that His Word is true. We have to see through eyes of faith and not a glass of fear. Hindrances will come and they come to discourage us and to take us into a place of fear and doubt but we have to keep our minds stayed on the promises of God no matter what situation we find ourselves in. We have to trust God and His Word at all times so that we can stay in a place where our faith will always shatter the glass of fear.

AS WE BEGIN TO SHATTER THE GLASS OF FEAR, <u>WE MUST UNDERSTAND</u> THAT ...

✷ Hindrances can come in the form of people, places, and things. If there are people, places, and things that are causing you to walk contrary to the Word you know, avoid them. When something is contrary, it is noticeable because it is opposite in nature, meaning, and direction. It causes you to go the wrong way.

> *Romans 16:17*
> *Now I beseech you, brethren, mark them which cause divisions and offenses contrary to the doctrine which ye have learned; and avoid them.*

✻ No matter how much you have a desire to do something, there will be times when you will be hindered but you have to press on. Pressing on requires force. There is a steady push that counteracts the pressure you are facing when you press on. The force and the push of pressing on is what will help you to shatter the glass of fear in your life.

> *I Thessalonians 2:18*
> *Wherefore we would have come unto you, even I Paul, once and again; but Satan hindered us.*

✻ Anything that keeps you from trusting and believing God with your whole heart is a hindrance. Fear and doubt are hindrances to your faith. We have to fear NOT and we have to doubt NOT if we are to fully walk in faith.

> *Isaiah 41:10*
> *Fear thou not; for I am with thee: be not dismayed; for I am thy God: I will strengthen thee; yea, I will help thee; yea, I will uphold thee with the right hand of my righteousness.*

AS YOU SHATTER THE GLASS OF FEAR IN YOUR LIFE, <u>ASK YOURSELF</u> ...

What is in your way? What is proving to be a glass of fear in your life? What is blocking you mentally, spiritually, and/or physically and keeping you from completely putting your faith, hope, and trust in God?

ACTION STEP: Cast down all fear and doubt as soon as it enters your mind! The Bible tells us to cast down every thought that exalts itself against the knowledge of God. Fear and doubt take root in your heart and mind and begin to grow from there. So you have to pluck up and cast down fear and doubt as soon as it comes into your heart and your mind.

Write down 3 statements of faith that you will speak over your life when fear comes and tries to infiltrate your heart and mind in an effort to hinder your faith. For example, when fear says, I am not good enough. My statement of faith that I will speak over my life will say, "I am a child of God. I was created in His image and after His likeness and I am not just good enough, I am more than enough because the Spirit of God dwells within me".

> *2 Corinthians 10:5*
> *Casting down imaginations, and every high thing that exalteth itself against the knowledge of God, and bringing into captivity every thought to the obedience of Christ;*

Whether you write it here, in a journal, or on another piece of paper, take time to write down the answers to the following:

1) _____
   _____
   _____
   _____

2) _____
   _____
   _____
   _____

3) _____
   _____
   _____
   _____

CONFESSION

Father today I uproot, bind up, and cast down every thought that has entered my mind that is not in line with what You have said about me and promised me. I know today that fear is not my portion. I know that You are well able to do whatever needs to be done in my life. My hope, my faith, and my trust are all in You. You are the Creator of all things. You are God alone and I will not doubt the

Word that You have already placed on the inside of me. Today Father I will walk fully in faith and I will speak to the hindrances in my life that are causing me to live behind the glass of fear. I speak to every hindering force and I say be removed now because my faith, my hope, and my trust are all in God and He is well able to bring to pass everything that I have need of in my life.

STOP
TAKE TIME TO MEDITATE ON WHAT YOU HAVE READ, THE QUESTIONS YOU HAVE ANSWERED, AND THE STEPS YOU HAVE TAKEN BEFORE PROCEEDING TO THE NEXT CHAPTER OF THIS BOOK.

Chapter 8
WHAT IT MEANS TO HAVE UNWAVERING FAITH

The word wavering means to move in a quivering way. It means to become weaker and to falter. It means to stumble. When we waver we tend to fluctuate our allegiance and our dependence on who and/or what we say we believe. To waver means to weave and to sway from one direction to another[1] and that is not how our faith should be. Our faith has to be steadfast and unmovable because with faith comes pressure, tests, trials, and attacks. The enemy is going to do everything within his power to cause you to become weak in your faith so that you can remain behind the glass of fear but you have to stand and stay strong under the pressure that comes with life and the only way you can stand and stay strong is by fully walking in faith.

The thing about fear is that it is not only an emotion, it is also a reaction. Fear is an emotion that is usually triggered

---

[1] dictionary.com

by the feeling that something will happen to you or something won't happen for you and it also is a reaction or a response to something that has happened to you. We have to be diligent and make sure we are casting down the very thought of fear when the thought arises and we have to counteract the feeling of fear with the Word of God. God tells us throughout His Word to fear not but we have to read, understand, and know His Word in order for us to do what He has said in His Word. If you never take time to learn what the Word tells you to do in response to fear, you will never know what to do. It is my prayer that this book will help give you a jumpstart and some insight on how to counteract the spirit of fear in and over your life.

AS WE BEGIN TO SHATTER THE GLASS OF FEAR, <u>WE MUST UNDERSTAND</u> THAT ...

❋ God has told us to fear NOT. When we are told not to do something, that means we are prohibited from doing it. It means we should refuse to do it. God does not want us to live behind the glass of fear or even walk in fear. He has already told us that He is with us. He said He is our God and He will strengthen us. He said that He would help us and uphold us. So why should we fear?

> *Isaiah 41:10*
> *Fear thou not; for I am with thee: be not dismayed; for I am thy God: I will strengthen thee; yea, I will help thee; yea, I will uphold thee with the right hand of My righteousness.*

✵ Unwavering faith requires us to be steadfast and unmovable. When you are steadfast and unmovable, you are spiritually anchored to and with God. You are not in a constant emotional whirlwind. Your thoughts and your emotions are rooted and grounded in the Word of God.

> *I Corinthians 15:58*
> *Therefore, my beloved brethren, be ye stedfast, unmoveable, always abounding in the work of the Lord, forasmuch as ye know that your labour is not in vain in the Lord.*

✵ God wants us to hold fast to our faith without wavering. In other words, He wants us to cling to our faith. He doesn't want us constantly letting go of what we say we believe or what we say we are believing Him for.

> *Hebrews 10:23*
> *Let us hold fast the profession of our faith without wavering; (for He is faithful that promised;)*

AS YOU SHATTER THE GLASS OF FEAR IN YOUR LIFE, ASK YOURSELF ...

Are you holding on to your faith even when things get hard and it looks like what you are believing God for is not coming to pass?

ACTION STEP: Gird yourself up with the Word of God. When you are girded up, you are secure and surrounded. Our security is only in and with God and our mind has to be secure and full of the Word of God.

Take a moment and write down 3 scriptures that deal with waiting on God and/or having unwavering faith in God.

> *1 Peter 1:13*
> *Wherefore gird up the loins of your mind, be sober, and hope to the end for the grace that is to be brought unto you at the revelation of Jesus Christ;*

Whether you write it here, in a journal, or on another piece of paper, take time to write down your answers.

1) _____
_____
_____
_____

2) _____
   _____
   _____
   _____

3) _____
   _____
   _____
   _____

CONFESSION

Father today I stand strong in You. I declare and I decree that I will not live behind the glass of fear and I will not waver in faith. Today I gird up my mind with Your Word that says You know the things I have need of and You are faithful and just to provide me with those things. Father today I bind up and I cast down every thought that is trying to exalt itself against what You have already said to be true. You said that You would watch over me, shield me, protect me, heal me, and provide for me. Your Word stands and I am standing on Your Word. Thank You Father for always making a way for me and for surrounding me with Your love, peace, power, provision, and protection. I will not waver when it comes to trusting and believing that You will honor Your Word in my life. I shall walk fully in faith in Jesus name ... amen.

STOP

TAKE TIME TO MEDITATE ON WHAT YOU HAVE READ, THE QUESTIONS YOU HAVE ANSWERED, AND THE STEPS YOU HAVE TAKEN BEFORE PROCEEDING TO THE NEXT CHAPTER OF THIS BOOK.

Chapter 9
A MEASURE OF FAITH

One of the things we must establish upfront is what it says in 2 Thessalonians 3:2. We have to understand that that the Bible says "not all men have faith". Unreasonable and wicked men are not men of faith. How can you have faith in God if you don't honor Him, respect Him, and believe in Him? Furthermore, to have something means you take ownership of it. It means you accept something, you receive it, your retain it, and you implement it. You have it in your possession and you use it at your discretion. Faith says that you believe God. It says that your trust is in God to do what He said He would do. It means you receive His Word as your own and you hold on to it and believe that God will honor His Word in your life.

Wicked men do not follow God because their trust and their hope is not in what God can do. They have not received God's Word as true. Not only have they not received it, they don't retain it, and they have not taken ownership of it. Yes, the Bible says that God has given every man the measure of faith but just because a person receives a portion of something, doesn't mean they will take ownership of it and how they use it or not use it is up to them. When you take ownership of something, you accept the responsibility that comes with it. You become accountable for it. Wicked men don't want to be responsible or accountable for having faith in God.

Let's take a moment and talk about the meaning of the word measure. One definition for measure means to ascertain the size, amount, or degree of something by using an instrument or device. Another definition for measure says it is a plan or course of action taken to achieve a particular purpose.[2] Let's consider the second definition and understand, God has given His people a plan and a course of action to achieve His purpose in the earth through faith and the more we believe Him and the stronger our faith is in Him, the more we can achieve for Him. Wicked men are not looking to achieve anything for God. Although God has given them a measure of faith, they don't have faith because they have not taken ownership or possession of it because they know with faith comes purpose and the purpose of faith is to please God. Remember, without faith it is impossible to please God. Wicked men are not looking to bring pleasure to God. We have to remember it is the measure of faith that God has given us that will in essence help us to break the glass of fear and walk fully in faith as long as we receive it from God and implement it in our walk with Him.

---

[2] dictionary.com

AS WE BEGIN TO SHATTER THE GLASS OF FEAR, <u>WE MUST UNDERSTAND</u> THAT ...

✷ The measure of faith is given by God to all men but not all men have faith because they have not taken possession of what they have been given. They have not taken ownership of God's Word. With ownership comes power, authority, and dominion and that is what God wants us to have and utilize in the earth. He wants us to have dominion and He wants us to exercise His power and His authority and we can only do that by walking in faith and having complete trust in His Word.

> *Romans 12:3*
> *For I say, through the grace given unto me, to every man that is among you, not to think of himself more highly than he ought to think; but to think soberly, according as God hath dealt to every man the measure of faith.*

> *2 Thessalonians 3:1-3*
> *Finally, brethren, pray for us, that the word of the Lord may have free course, and be glorified, even as it is with you: And that we may be delivered from unreasonable and wicked men: for all men have not faith. But the Lord is faithful, who shall stablish you, and keep you from evil.*

AS YOU SHATTER THE GLASS OF FEAR IN YOUR LIFE, ASK YOURSELF ...

Are you operating in the measure of faith that God has given you? Whether it be defined as the degree (amount, level, or extent) of faith or defined as the plan and course of action that God has given you to achieve His purpose in the earth? We have to operate in the faith that God has given us in order for us to do all that He has called us to do.

ACTION STEP: Look up the word measure. Look at the definition as if you are using the word as a verb and also look at the definition as if you are using it as a noun. The Bible says God has given us "the measure" of faith. Meditate on the meaning of the word in every context.

> *Romans 12:3*
> *For I say, through the grace given unto me, to every man that is among you, not to think of himself more highly than he ought to think; but to think soberly, according as God hath dealt to every man the measure of faith.*

Whether you write it here, in a journal, or on another piece of paper, take time to write down the answers to the following:

1) Noun Meaning Of The Word "Measure"

_____
_____
_____

2) Verb Meaning Of The Word "Measure"

_____
_____
_____
_____

CONFESSION

    Father thank You for giving me the measure of faith. It is by faith that I shall be able to shatter the glass of fear in and over my life. Father I take ownership of Your Word. I will allow Your Word to lead me, guide me, and direct me in life. Father my faith is in You and what You have said You would do. You are my constant companion and Your Word shall have free rein in and over my life. Father today I declare and decree that I have faith. I take ownership of the Word that You have placed on the inside of me. I will take dominion and exercise the authority and power that You have given me. I will represent You well as I walk fully in faith in Jesus name ... amen.

STOP

TAKE TIME TO MEDITATE ON WHAT YOU HAVE READ, THE QUESTIONS YOU HAVE ANSWERED, AND THE STEPS YOU HAVE TAKEN BEFORE PROCEEDING TO THE NEXT CHAPTER OF THIS BOOK.

Chapter 10
HOW FAITH COMES

When you look at life and people in this life that are walking by faith, have you ever wondered, how did they get so much faith? How did they get to the point where they trust God completely? The place where the glass of fear doesn't seem to have a hold on them. The place where the Word always tends to override the worry in their lives. That is the place where God wants us all to be. He wants us to be in a place where our faith in Him is not shaken or moved when things seem to be going in a different direction than the one He has promised.

Faith is not automatic. It does not automatically take over when we are faced with challenges in life. That is why the Bible tells us to build up ourselves on our most holy faith. It tells us to stand strong in faith, to walk by faith, and to live by faith. Let's think about what faith is. It is COMPLETE trust and COMPLETE confidence in God. When something is complete, it has everything that is necessary to make it work. The only way to make our faith work is if it is based COMPLETELY on God and His Word. So we have to know how faith comes. The Bible says that faith comes by hearing and what we are hearing has to come from the Word of God. God's Word is complete and we have to have complete trust and confidence in it.

AS WE BEGIN TO SHATTER THE GLASS OF FEAR, <u>WE MUST UNDERSTAND</u> THAT ...

✳ Who and what we listen to does matter. The words that we let enter our hearts and minds can encourage us or they can discourage us. Be conscious of the voice and the words that you are allowing to be spoken into and over your life. Make sure they are are words that coincide with God's Word and strengthen your faith.

> *Proverbs 15:4*
> *A wholesome tongue [is] a tree of life: but perverseness therein [is] a breach in the spirit.*

✳ We have to hear God's Word in order for faith to come. Hearing means we are to perceive, catch, discern, and distinguish the sound of something. We have to be able to discern what God is saying to us through His Word. Many voices will speak to us but it is only God's voice that can save us and build up our faith.

> *John 10:27*
> *My sheep hear my voice, and I know them,*
> *and they follow me:*

AS YOU SHATTER THE GLASS OF FEAR IN YOUR LIFE, <u>ASK YOURSELF</u> ...

Are you taking the time each day to build yourself up in faith by reading God's Word and listening to it? Listening to God's Word can include listening to a message, listening to the Bible online, listening to praise and worship, talking to someone about God, etc.

ACTION STEP: Try to make sure God's voice is the first voice you seek to hear in the morning and the last voice you try to hear each day whether it be by Him speaking to you through His written Word, through prayer, through worship, from a conversation, or from an audible preached message. Try to let your first conversation in the morning be prayer, knowing that prayer is a conversation with God and let your last words at night be words of thanksgiving to God.

> *Romans 10:17*
> *So then faith cometh by hearing, and hearing by the Word of God.*

CONFESSION

Father thank You for Your Word. Today I commit to staying in Your Word. It is my desire to hear from You. Father You are God and Your Word are truth. I want to know You and I want to live according to Your Word. I commit now to reading Your Word, praying Your Word, hearing Your Word, discerning Your Word, and living my life according to Your Word. Father I will guard my Spirit and I will be conscious and aware of what I allow into the ear gates and eye gates of my soul. I will make sure that what I allow to come in will prove to be spiritual nourishment and cause me to walk strong in faith with You in Jesus name ... amen.

STOP

TAKE TIME TO MEDITATE ON WHAT YOU HAVE READ, THE QUESTIONS YOU HAVE ANSWERED, AND THE STEPS YOU HAVE TAKEN BEFORE PROCEEDING TO THE NEXT CHAPTER OF THIS BOOK.

Chapter 11
HOW TO DEVELOP YOUR FAITH

When you develop something it grows and it becomes more mature. It becomes clearer over a process of time. God wants us to have mature faith. God wants your faith to go through the process of growth over the process of time until you become spiritually mature. When something or someone is mature, it reflects different qualities and different characteristics. God wants us to no longer display the characteristics of fear. There are things that cause fear in your life when you are a baby in faith that should no longer be able to cause you anxiety as you grow in faith. As we grow and our characteristics change, we have to understand that God wants us to be able to look at our lives and see the glass of fear shattered. He wants to see us fully walking in faith because when we walk fully in faith we are saying that our hope, trust, and confidence are all in Him.

Being a mature Christian and walking in mature faith is not based on a person's age and it is not based on how long a person has been saved. Being a mature Christian is based on the Word you know and how you implement that Word in your life. There are many people that know the Word of God and never implement it. When you implement something, you put it into action and you use it for a particular purpose. As we grow in God, we should be growing in a way that helps us to not only know God's Word but we should be able to apply God's Word to our lives.

What we must understand as our faith matures is that our faith has to be nourished. Nourishment is important to the growth process. Think about a child. One of the most important factors that affects growth and immunity in a child is nourishment and nourishment comes through a balanced diet. It is the same with faith. We have to feed our faith and our faith has to be nourished by the Word of God. It is only after we nourish our faith and cause our faith to grow that we become spiritually mature in faith and at that point we are strong enough to break the glass of fear and withstand the attacks of the enemy. At that point we have the stamina to stand and wait on God.

AS WE BEGIN TO SHATTER THE GLASS OF FEAR, <u>WE MUST UNDERSTAND</u> THAT …

* You have to be strong in the Lord and the power of His might in order to stand and stay in faith. One of the reasons we need to be strong in the Lord is because in our weakness, God is still strong. So at that point we cannot be overtaken by trials that come with life. There is nothing the enemy can ever bring against your life that can overpower God's plan for Your life. You just have to

make sure that you are living your life according to God's plan and not your own.

> *Ephesians 6:10-12*
> *Finally, my brethren, be strong in the Lord, and in the power of his might. Put on the whole armour of God, that ye may be able to stand against the wiles of the devil. For we wrestle not against flesh and blood, but against principalities, against powers, against the rulers of the darkness of this world, against spiritual wickedness in high places.*

* In order to be spiritually mature, we must grow in the knowledge of who God is and what Jesus did. Growth with God is a process that is never ending. So we should never be at a point where we fail to grow spiritually stronger with God.

> *2 Peter 3:18*
> *But grow in grace, and [in] the knowledge of our Lord and Saviour Jesus Christ. To Him [be] glory both now and for ever. Amen*

AS YOU SHATTER THE GLASS OF FEAR IN YOUR LIFE, ASK YOURSELF ...

What word or words are you snacking on throughout the day to keep yourself encouraged? Healthy snacks are important for our growth and the question is are you snacking on the Word of God throughout the day or are you snacking on the junk food of the world by opening up your heart, ears, and mind to everything that is going on in the world?

ACTION STEP: Make sure you are snacking and feasting on the Word of God. Take time to read and meditate on God's Word today. Write down 3 short scriptures that you can snack on during the day to encourage yourself in faith.

> *Amos 8:11*
> *Behold, the days come, saith the Lord GOD, that I will send a famine in the land, not a famine of bread, nor a thirst for water, but of hearing the words of the LORD:*

Whether you write it here, in a journal, or on another piece of paper, take time to write down your answers:

1) _____
   _____
   _____
   _____

2) _____
   _____
   _____
   _____

3) _____
   _____
   _____
   _____

CONFESSION

Father today I will feast on Your Word. I know that You have prepared a table for me in the presence of my enemies and I will take a seat at that table knowing that You are with me. Father Your Word is truth and I will speak Your Word and declare and decree Your Word in the earth. I shall grow strong in You. Father Your Holy Spirit dwells on the inside of me and I know greater are You in me than anything I am coming up against in this world. God You have given me the measure of faith and I will develop in the faith that You have given me. I will develop to the point that I no longer will be seen hiding behind a glass of fear but I will be seen fully walking in faith in Jesus name ... amen.

STOP
TAKE TIME TO MEDITATE ON WHAT YOU HAVE READ, THE QUESTIONS YOU HAVE ANSWERED, AND THE STEPS YOU HAVE TAKEN BEFORE PROCEEDING TO THE NEXT CHAPTER OF THIS BOOK.

Chapter 12
FAITH IN GOD TAKES AWAY THE PRIDE OF SELF

Think about what it means to have your faith in God knowing that you can do nothing in and by yourself. We have to know that it is in God that we live, breathe, and have our being. We couldn't even breathe without God and yet there are many people who walk in pride thinking that what they have achieved, they have done it without the hand or the help of God Almighty.

Pride is rooted in self-will as opposed to God's will. We all should be living in a way that is asking God for His will to be done in us, for us, and through us. We can only do that when we know what our purpose in life is. We have been purposed to fulfill God's will on the earth. THAT IS OUR PURPOSE and we can only fulfill that purpose by moving beyond the glass of fear and walking fully in faith!

The thing about self-will is it doesn't care about the opinions, wishes, or orders of others. We can say that it is ruthless. When something or someone is ruthless, they have no pity or compassion for others. Compassion is rooted in love and God is love. The root of everything we do needs to be in God and the love of God. We need to be living our lives in a way that says to God, "not my will but Thy will be done". Our lives should always display who God is and what He would have us to do.

AS WE BEGIN TO SHATTER THE GLASS OF FEAR, <u>WE MUST UNDERSTAND</u> THAT ...

✳ Even in the hard times we need to be asking God for His will to be done in our lives just as Jesus did. It is not easy to always adhere to what God is asking us to do. Sometimes our choices can be very complicated but we still have to make the right choice and that choice should always be based on our desire to fulfill the will of God.

> *Luke 22:42*
> *Saying, Father, if thou be willing, remove this cup from me: nevertheless not my will, but thine, be done.*

✳ Conforming our lives to the Word of God and not the ways of the world helps us to prove the will of God. When you conform to something, you act in accordance with the standards and the expectations of what you are conforming to. So when we conform our lives to God's Word, we act in accordance to the standards that God has given us in His Word. God's Word becomes our guideline.

> *Romans 12:2*
> *And be not conformed to this world: but be ye transformed by the renewing of your mind, that ye may prove what [is] that good, and acceptable, and perfect, will of God.*

* Pride is deceitful. It has a person believing something that is not true. God and His Word are true and because pride promotes deceit, we know that it is not in alignment with what God has said or what God would have us to do.

> *Galatians 6:3*
> *For if a man think himself to be something, when he is nothing, he deceiveth himself.*

* God hates pride and the attitude and actions that go with it. Pride is an attitude that is rooted in "self". It is an attitude of self-importance, self-reliance, self-love, and self-exaltation. These are all reasons that contributed to satan being kicked out of heaven. We should never be so confident in self that we see ourselves as more important than God or even others. There is a limit to confidence. We need to make sure our confidence is confidence in God and not self. Everything we are able to do is only by God's grace, love, and mercy.

> *Proverbs 8:13*
> *The fear of the LORD [is] to hate evil: pride, and arrogancy, and the evil way, and the froward mouth, do I hate.*

AS YOU SHATTER THE GLASS OF FEAR IN YOUR LIFE, <u>ASK YOURSELF</u> ...

Are you walking in pride concerning the things you have achieved in life or are you thanking God for the things you have been able to achieve and saying to God, not my will but thy will be done and meaning it?

ACTION STEP: Make sure you are giving God praise and not seeking the praise of the people around you. Take a moment and explain how the enemy can try to trap you in order to gain praise for the things that God is doing for you and your family in the following scenarios. Write down how you would divert the attention back to God?

> *Psalm 150*
> *Praise ye the Lord. Praise God in His sanctuary: praise Him in the firmament of His power. Praise Him for His mighty acts: praise Him according to His excellent greatness. Praise Him with the sound of the trumpet: praise Him with the psaltery and harp. Praise Him with the timbrel and dance: praise Him with stringed instruments and organs. Praise Him upon the loud cymbals: praise Him upon the high sounding cymbals. Let every thing that hath breath praise the Lord.*
> *Praise ye the Lord.*

Whether you write it here, in a journal, or on another piece of paper, take time to write down your answers:

1) You receive a promotion at work.

_____
_____
_____
_____
_____
_____
_____

2) You get a new car.

_____
_____
_____
_____

3) Your children are acknowledged for a special achievement.

CONFESSION

Father today as I walk fully in faith, I walk forward knowing that it is only in You that I live, breathe, and I have my being. Father, You are worthy to be praised. Today I bind up self. Father I do not want to be self-reliant. I choose to be reliant on You. I do not want to be self-important. I know that there is nothing or no one more important than You. Father the love I have for myself will never outweigh the love I have for You. Thank You Father for helping me to know who I am in and with You. Today Father, I bind up and I cast down any and every opportunity that may arise in my life to try to persuade me to walk in pride. If there be anything in me that is operating in my life right now that is unlike You, I bind it up and cast it down right now. Father, great is your love for me and great is Your faithfulness. I know that there is nothing that I can do without You. So right now Father I say thank You. Thank You for what You have done, what You are doing, and what You will do in and through my life in Jesus name ... amen.

STOP
TAKE TIME TO MEDITATE ON WHAT YOU HAVE READ, THE QUESTIONS YOU HAVE ANSWERED, AND THE STEPS YOU HAVE TAKEN BEFORE PROCEEDING TO THE NEXT CHAPTER OF THIS BOOK.

Chapter 13
SAVING FAITH

What is it that you believe? Do you believe once saved always saved even if your life and lifestyle go against God's Word, His Will, and His Way? Do you believe in God but don't truly believe in the birth, death, and resurrection of Jesus? Is your personal trust and reliance on God and in His Word? There is no way to move beyond the glass of fear if your faith and your belief are not fully in God.

A lot of people say a lot of things but don't believe half of what they say themselves. There are many people that say the salvation prayer and they have confessed Jesus as their Lord and Savior and yet they doubt the truth of what they said. They also doubt whether or not God will move on their behalf just as He did for Jesus. You cannot walk fully in faith if you are in constant doubt and fear as to whether or not God can or will move on your behalf. Understand, your salvation is based on your belief and if you don't believe in Jesus and the work that He did, you can't be saved by Him. True saving faith not only confesses Jesus as Lord and Savior, it believes that Jesus is our Lord and

Savior. We also have to understand it takes more than just believing that Jesus is our Lord and Savior. The Bible tells us that even the demons believe. We have to not only believe, we also have to put our trust in Him as our Lord and Savior and that can only be done by faith.

The disciples and men of old had Jesus with them and yet some of them had a hard time walking fully in faith. They saw the miracles first hand and yet Jesus called them out for having little faith and He even asked them where was their faith. Don't be that person that has seen the hand of God move in miraculous ways in your life and the lives of others and yet you fail to walk fully in faith. Don't be one of the ones who has questionable faith. When something is questionable, it is open to doubt and it can be challenged. Don't give the enemy the tool of doubt so that he can question your faith and cause you to question your God.

Saving faith does just what it says. It saves you. It is the faith that you have in Jesus. Saving faith is essential. It is the foundation of biblical faith. Saving faith says that you believe in your heart and you have a personal conviction that Jesus was born, died, and resurrected for you. Saving faith goes beyond just mental assent. Saving faith causes you to repent and it causes you to put your complete trust and belief in the Savior. Saving faith hears the Word of God, believes the Word of God, and acts upon the Word of God. Even when things don't work out as expected, saving faith keeps you rooted and grounded in the promises of God because you know that you have a Savior and you are covered by the blood.

AS WE BEGIN TO SHATTER THE GLASS OF FEAR, <u>WE MUST UNDERSTAND</u> THAT ...

* It is by grace that we are saved through faith and our salvation is the gift of God. You have to remember that a gift is given. It is something that is bestowed upon you and it is something you don't have to pay for. Salvation is a gift to us from God that Jesus paid the price for but we have to receive the gift of salvation by faith.

> *Ephesians 2:8-9*
> *For by grace are ye saved through faith; and that not of yourselves: it is the gift of God: Not of works, lest any man should boast.*

* Saving faith causes you to hunger and thirst for righteousness because you begin to realize that Jesus is the bread of life and He is the living water. When you are truly hungry and thirsty, you seek food and you seek drink. You seek to be filled. God wants us to hunger and to thirst for righteousness. In other words, He wants us to seek Him and to be full of Him so that our desire for righteousness (righteous living) will outweigh our desire for sin.

> *John 6:35*
> *And Jesus said unto them, I am the bread of life: he that cometh to me shall never hunger; and he that believeth on me shall never thirst.*

AS YOU SHATTER THE GLASS OF FEAR IN YOUR LIFE, ASK YOURSELF ...

Have you gone beyond mental assent and have you asked Jesus to come into your life and to be your Lord and Savior? Do you truly believe in the works of the Lord?

ACTION STEP: Make sure your hunger and thirst are for righteousness and not the ways of man. Take time to write down 5 scriptures that you will call your "Food For Thought". Scriptures that talk about the Word of God being spiritual food.

> *Matthew 5:6*
> *Blessed are they which do hunger and thirst after righteousness: for they shall be filled.*

Whether you write it here, in a journal, or on another piece of paper, take time to write down the answers.

1) _____

2) _____

_____
_____

3) _____
_____
_____
_____

4) _____
_____
_____
_____

5) _____
_____
_____
_____

CONFESSION

Father I believe that you are real and because I believe you are real, I take a stand on You and Your Word. I believe that Jesus is my Lord and Savior. I believe that He was born, died, and resurrected for me. I believe that I can do all things in, through, and with Christ. I believe! Father not only do I believe, I am hungry and I thirst for Your righteousness. Father show me Your ways. Fill me with Your Word. Quench my thirst with Your living water. I no longer want to have a hunger for the things of the world.

For Jesus is the bread of life and He is Your Word made flesh. Today and everyday I want to feast on Your Word. I know that my strength comes from You. Nourish my soul so that my thoughts are stayed on You. Help me Father to be filled with the fruit of who You are to the point that I overflow and let the overflow of who and what You are flow over from my life into and onto the lives of those whom You have placed around me in Jesus name ... amen.

STOP
TAKE TIME TO MEDITATE ON WHAT YOU HAVE READ, THE QUESTIONS YOU HAVE ANSWERED, AND THE STEPS YOU HAVE TAKEN BEFORE PROCEEDING TO THE NEXT CHAPTER OF THIS BOOK.

Chapter 14
SUSTAINING FAITH

To sustain means to strengthen and support physically as well as mentally. It means to undergo or suffer something unpleasant but to keep going.[3] God wants us to have the kind of faith that sustains us in the midst of trials, tribulation, and just everyday life.

Life is not always going to be easy. We will come up against situations that challenge our faith. Our faith may be saying God will do a thing and our situation may be saying just the opposite. We have to have the type of faith that refuses to give up or give in to outward circumstances. We have to have the faith that can undergo the sufferings that life in this world will bring and still stay strong. The kind of faith that sustains you has to be rooted and grounded in the Word of God because His promises are true and His Word stands the test of time and the challenges that come with time. We have to have the kind of faith that doesn't stand or stay behind the glass of fear

---

[3] dictionary.com

when challenges come but instead moves forward with God knowing that He is in complete control even when life feels out of control.

Sustaining faith is just that. It is the faith that sustains you. The faith that won't let you give up no matter how hard your situation appears to be. The faith that will believe God's Word no matter what. The kind of faith that energizes you and supports your righteous cause.

Sustaining faith is relentless. It is unending and unceasing. It is not sporadic. It believes non-stop. Sustaining faith is persistent, constant, and steady. If you are walking in faith, these traits of sustaining faith should be seen clearly in your walk.

AS WE BEGIN TO SHATTER THE GLASS OF FEAR, <u>WE MUST UNDERSTAND</u> THAT ...

* In order to walk in sustaining faith, you must first trust God, obey God, and patiently wait on God. Remember to sustain means to be strengthened and supported and our strength and support both come from God and His Word.

> *Psalms 18:32*
> *It is God that girdeth me with strength, and maketh my way perfect.*

✳ Sustaining faith helps you to overcome challenges. It keeps you even when feel like giving up. In order to fully walk in the kind of faith that sustains you, you have to be rooted, grounded, and settled in what you say you believe.

> *Colossians 1:23*
> *If ye continue in the faith grounded and settled, and be not moved away from the hope of the gospel, which ye have heard, and which was preached to every creature which is under heaven; whereof I Paul am made a minister;*

AS YOU SHATTER THE GLASS OF FEAR IN YOUR LIFE, ASK YOURSELF ...

Are you walking in sustaining faith? In other words, are rooted and grounded in God's Word to the point that you allow your faith to sustain and anchor you when you are faced with opposition in life? Is your faith supporting you, holding you up, and helping you to shatter the glass of fear concerning your situation?

ACTION STEP: Check your foundation. Make sure your foundation is sure. To have faith that sustains you, you need to have a strong word base that teaches you to trust, obey, and to wait on God. Write out 3 scriptures today. One on trusting God, one on obeying God, and one on waiting on God.

> *Isaiah 40:31*
> *But they that wait upon the LORD shall renew their strength; they shall mount up with wings as eagles; they shall run, and not be weary; and they shall walk, and not faint.*

Whether you write it here, in a journal, or on another piece of paper, take time to write down the answers.

1) Write down a scripture about trusting God.
_____
_____
_____
_____

2) Write down a scripture about obeying God.
_____
_____
_____
_____

3) Write down a scripture about waiting on God.

_____
_____
_____

CONFESSION

Father thank You for giving me sustaining faith. Because I have sustaining faith, I am able to shatter the glass of fear in my life and walk fully in faith. I know Father that you are going to nourish me, nurture me, keep me, confirm me, affirm me, and take care of me. Father I trust You. Because I have faith, I am able to obey You. Because I have faith, I am able to wait on You. Your Word is true and Your Word is rooted and grounded in my heart. Father thank You for never leaving me and for never forsaking me. Thank You Father for Your unending love and for Your continual blessings. Father thank You for always honoring Your Word in my life in Jesus name ... amen.

STOP

TAKE TIME TO MEDITATE ON WHAT YOU HAVE READ, THE QUESTIONS YOU HAVE ANSWERED, AND THE STEPS YOU HAVE TAKEN BEFORE PROCEEDING TO THE NEXT CHAPTER OF THIS BOOK.

Chapter 15
WHAT FAITH BRINGS

Faith is trusting and believing that God will bring forth His promises in your life. In order for God to bring forth His promises, you have to first know what He has promised you. Do you know what God has promised you in and through His Word? So often we say we are standing on the promises of God but the true question is, do you really know what He has promised you?

The only way way to shatter the glass of fear and walk fully in God's Word is to know what God has promised in His Word to do for you, in you, and through you. The Word of God is described as a firm foundation. When something is firm, it is solid and unyielding. That is what the Word of God is. It is a solid foundation that doesn't yield, cave in, or give way to the pressures that come with life. That is why it is important for your faith to be in God and His Word because it is the foundation on which you must stand.

Your faith has to be unyielding. Your faith should not give way to the pressures, arguments, and demands that come with life in this world. That means your faith needs to remain strong in the midst of the trials that come with life. So often in life it is the fear that tends to be unyielding and people walk around with shattered faith. Remember, God wants us to shatter the glass of fear and to walk fully in faith.

In order for your faith to remain strong, you have to be sure in who and what you say you trust and believe. So if you say you trust and believe in God and His promises, you have to know Him and His promises. How can you trust in who and what you do not know? The mere fact that you don't know someone or something brings in the elements of doubt and fear. When you think about faith bringing forth God's promises, you have to not only know God's promises are true, you have to trust and believe that He is a Man of His Word and His Word is the Truth.

As we think about the promises of God, we have to know that God has promised us eternal life. We have to know that if God's Word abides in us, and if we have surrendered our lives to Him and invited Jesus in as our Lord and Savior, we have eternal life. It takes faith to believe that. It takes faith to believe we have a Savior that was born, died, and raised from the dead for our sins. We have to have faith because without faith, we can't have eternal life.

Another promise that God has given us is that He will never leave us nor forsake us. So we can walk boldly knowing that He is with us and we are never alone. There are many more promises in God's Word. We have to know and stand on each and every one of them. When we stand on the promises of God, we are standing on what we know our faith will bring. We are standing on our firm foundation.

AS WE BEGIN TO SHATTER THE GLASS OF FEAR, <u>WE MUST UNDERSTAND</u> THAT ...

✸ Standing on God's promises helps us to escape the corruption and the lust of the world. We escape the lust of the world when we become partakers of God's divine nature. When you partake of something, you are a part of it. God wants us to partake of His divine nature so that we can escape the lust of the world. God's divine nature is a part of our salvation. It is what produces holy conduct and holy behavior. It is what keeps us from participating in the activities that are considered to be a part of the lust of the world.

> *2 Peter 1:3-4*
> *According as his divine power hath given unto us all things that pertain unto life and godliness, through the knowledge of Him that hath called us to glory and virtue: Whereby are given unto us exceeding great and precious promises: that by these ye might be partakers of the divine nature, having escaped the corruption that is in the world through lust.*

✳ Standing on God's promises helps you to be content with the things you have because you know that God is with you and He has promised to never leave you nor forsake you.

> *Hebrews 13:5-6*
> *Let your conversation be without covetousness; and be content with such things as ye have: for he hath said, I will never leave thee, nor forsake thee. So that we may boldly say, The Lord is my helper, and I will not fear what man shall do unto me.*

AS YOU SHATTER THE GLASS OF FEAR IN YOUR LIFE, ASK YOURSELF ...

Are you wavering in faith or are you standing steadfast and immovable on what God has said that He will do for you? Are you anchored to the promises of God? Are you content with what God has given you, knowing that He is still with you and whatever else you need in life, He is there to supply?

ACTION STEP: Take time to write out 5 promises that God has given you in His Word. Read them and meditate on them for the next 5 days.

> *Psalm 77:12-14*
> *I will meditate also of all thy work, and talk of thy doings. Thy way, O God, is in the sanctuary: who is so great a God as our God? Thou art the God that doest wonders: thou hast declared thy strength among the people.*

Whether you write it here, in a journal, or on another piece of paper, take time to write down the answers.

1) _____

2) _____

3) _____

4) _____

5) _____
_____
_____
_____

CONFESSION

Father today I stand on the promises that You have given me in Your Word. I know that You said that You will never leave me nor forsake me. You said that You would watch over Your Word to perform it in my life. You said that if I trust You and obey You, I will eat the good of the land. Thank You Father for every promise You have given me. I know Father that as I stand on Your promises I shall escape the corruption of the world. The lust of the world shall not have a hold on me. I shall be full of faith and the glass of fear shall be shattered in my life. I shall be strong in You in Jesus name ... amen.

STOP

TAKE TIME TO MEDITATE ON WHAT YOU HAVE READ, THE QUESTIONS YOU HAVE ANSWERED, AND THE STEPS YOU HAVE TAKEN BEFORE PROCEEDING TO THE NEXT CHAPTER OF THIS BOOK.

Chapter 16
WHAT IT MEANS TO HAVE MISPLACED FAITH

What is faith to you? Who is it or what is it that you have complete trust and confidence in? Is it God or is it the things that appear to be true in your own eyes? Are you giving more weight to those things you see or to the Word that God has said? When you give weight to something, you consider it to be more relevant and more important than something else. Nothing in your life should outweigh the Word of God for your life.

So often in life people misplace their faith. When you misplace something, you put it in the wrong place or you lose it. Understand, we can misplace our trust and our confidence by putting it in someone or something that we should not. When we take our trust and confidence away from God and put it on people, places, and things, we have misplaced our faith.

God wants our faith to be in Him. He wants us to trust and have total confidence in Him and in His Word. His Word should always outweigh the words that are being spoken by the people in the world around us. We can hear what others say but we must always remember that God's Word outweighs the words of man and God's Word should always have the final say in the situations concerning our lives.

Trusting in what God has said is not always easy to do because we have the gift of sight. That is why it is so easy to dwell behind the glass of fear. What we as people tend to do is rely on our sight more than what God has said. God has given us many things in life to help us on our journey. He has given us friends, family, doctors, jobs, homes, and cars. He has also given us leadership in our schools, churches, cities, states, and nations but none of the people, places, or things should ever override the voice and the Word of God in our lives. We cannot allow our trust and confidence to be moved or removed from God. We have to always remember that He is the source of life and all that we need in life is found in Him. Situations will come in an effort to cause us to be in fear but as we look at life through the window and lens of who God is and what He has promised to do, we stay focused and gain confidence in God and His promises and we stop letting fear cause us to fail when it comes to walking in faith.

AS WE BEGIN TO SHATTER THE GLASS OF FEAR, <u>WE MUST UNDERSTAND</u> THAT ...

✷ Trusting and having confidence in God and His Word will bring with it a reward. Patience and obedience will also set you up to receive the promises of God. One of the hardest things to do is to trust someone and have confidence in them. We have to know that God is trustworthy. He is worthy of our trust and we can be confident in His ability to do what He said He would do because He is the Creator of all things.

> *Hebrews 10:35-36*
> *Cast not away therefore your confidence, which hath great recompence of reward. For ye have need of patience, that, after ye have done the will of God, ye might receive the promise.*

✷ The world and people in the world are not always going to agree with you and what God has told you to do when you walk in faith with God but you can't allow your disagreement with the world and people in the world to hinder your trust, belief, and obedience to God.

> *Hebrews 11:7*
> *By faith Noah, being warned of God of things not seen as yet, moved with fear, prepared an ark to the saving of his house; by the which he condemned the world, and became heir of the righteousness which is by faith.*

* We have to take God at His Word because He has already told us the things that will come in order to mislead us. It is the devil's ultimate goal to mislead you and that is why it is important to know the promises of God so that you can quickly discern what is and what is not of God. Knowing the Word of God puts you in a position where you won't be easily tricked by the deceitfulness of the enemy.

> *Matthew 24:24*
> *For there shall arise false Christs, and false prophets, and shall shew great signs and wonders; insomuch that, if it were possible, they shall deceive the very elect.*

AS YOU SHATTER THE GLASS OF FEAR IN YOUR LIFE, ASK YOURSELF ...

Are you taking God at His Word even when your situation appears to be going against what He has said?

ACTION STEP: Rebuke fear and rebuttal it! Think about what happens when a defense attorney responds to the allegations by a district attorney. He rebuttals (denies, disapproves, and counteracts) what has been said. We have to do the same with fear. We have to counteract it by being determined to stay in faith and by speaking God's Word concerning the situations that are challenging our faith. How would you rebuttal the following situation if the enemy brought it up in an effort to cause you to walk in fear?

> Deuteronomy 31:6
> *Be strong and of a good courage, fear not, nor be afraid of them: for the LORD thy God, he [it is] that doth go with thee; he will not fail thee, nor forsake thee.*

Whether you write it here, in a journal, or on another piece of paper, take time to write down the answers .

1) What scripture reference would you give to rebuttal sickness and disease in your body? What would be your statement of faith in that situation?

_____
_____
_____
_____
_____
_____
_____
_____
_____
_____
_____
_____
_____
_____
_____

CONFESSION

Father today I rebuke fear. I stand in the face of fear and I declare and decree your promises to be true in and over my life. My faith is in You and not what I can see. I will not live my life behind the glass of fear. I shatter the glass that is before me that is hindering me from walking fully in faith and I will move forward with you. Father, I believe what You have said and I will stand firm on Your promises. My faith is in You and not in other people, places, or things. I will not be moved. I will not be misled. I will not put my faith in the words of men if they are not in alignment with Your Word. I am determined to stand on and obey You and Your Word in Jesus name ... amen.

STOP
TAKE TIME TO MEDITATE ON WHAT YOU HAVE READ, THE QUESTIONS YOU HAVE ANSWERED, AND THE STEPS YOU HAVE TAKEN BEFORE PROCEEDING TO THE NEXT CHAPTER OF THIS BOOK.

Chapter 17
LIMITED FAITH

Does your faith have limits? The glass of fear will limit your faith. Do you believe God to the point that you can conceive what you want or need? Do you believe that God can and will do the inconceivable in your life? To conceive means to form or develop.[4] Do you believe that God can create what you need if it does not already exist?

We have to trust and believe God beyond our own limitations and know that we serve a limitless God. Remember, fear is like glass. You can see through it but sometimes you have to break through it. The glass of fear will contain you and cause you to set boundaries concerning what you see, what you think, and what you believe that God can and/or will do for you. The glass of fear will cause you to put limitations on God.

When you are limited there are restrictions on what you can do. Understand, God is limitless but we can limit Him

---
[4] dictionary.com

by our faith.   There is no end to God.   There is no boundary to Him.   There is no limit to what He can do for us, in us, or through us.   We are the ones who limit God because we fail to walk fully in faith. We set boundaries for God and in essence tell Him what it is we believe He can do and in truth, HE CAN DO ALL THINGS.   We are so self-conscious that we put limits on the power of God being operative in our lives.   Understand being self-conscious means that we are aware of self. We need to move from being self-conscious where we are focused on what we can do and what we think God can do to being God conscious. We need to be focused on the supernatural power of God. We have to stop limiting God based on what we see and what we think. Instead, we need to fully surrender to God in faith so that we can see God do more in our lives than we can even imagine.   It is at that point we are shattering the glass of fear and moving fully in faith.

In the book of Matthew, the two blind men followed Jesus and cried out to Him asking Him to have mercy on them. Jesus' response was to touch their eyes and for their healing to be unto them according to their faith.   There are some things we won't be able to receive unless we have the faith to receive it. Think about the fact that the blind men could not see Jesus in the natural but they were able to receive their healing from Him because their faith expanded beyond the borders of their sight. They were not limited by the glass of fear or their inability to see. They had faith in the power of Jesus to the point that they were able to receive their sight.

AS WE BEGIN TO SHATTER THE GLASS OF FEAR, <u>WE MUST UNDERSTAND</u> THAT ...

✷ People tend to have faith in God to do some things in their lives but lack faith when it comes to Him doing other things. We must have faith in God for all things. Jesus is the author and finisher of our faith. He is the perfecter of our faith and because He is, we have to trust Him in every area of our lives for everything we need in life.

> *Hebrews 12:2*
> *Looking unto Jesus the author and finisher of our faith; who for the joy that was set before him endured the cross, despising the shame, and is set down at the right hand of the throne of God.*

AS YOU SHATTER THE GLASS OF FEAR IN YOUR LIFE, <u>ASK YOURSELF</u> ...

Are you failing to take every situation you are encountering in life to God for fear that He may not answer you? Do you feel that there are some things you can't accomplish on your own and yet you never seek God for the answer?

ACTION STEP: Take a moment to talk to God about everything you are encountering in your life right now no matter how small or how great the situation is. Write down 2 areas in your life that you really need God to move in. Surrender those 2 areas to God right now in prayer and have faith that He will do what only He can do.

> *1 Chronicles 16:11*
> *Seek the Lord and His strength;*
> *Seek His face continually.*

> *Hebrews 4:16*
> *"Let us therefore come boldly unto the throne of grace, that we may obtain mercy, and find grace to help in time of need."*

Whether you write it here, in a journal, or on another piece of paper, take time to write down the answers .

1) _____
   _____
   _____
   _____

2) _____
   _____
   _____
   _____

CONFESSION

Father You are God and my faith is in You alone. I know that I cannot accomplish anything in this life without You. So today I give You my all. I give You all of my heart and I give You all of the situations that are concerning me in life. Today I take the limits off that I have placed on You and I am determined to walk in limitless faith. Father I know that You will do in me, through me, and for me what only You can. I know that as I speak Your Word, my words are backed by You and Your Word. Today I not only walk in faith, I am walking in expectancy for You to honor Your Word and Your will in my life in Jesus name ... amen.

STOP

TAKE TIME TO MEDITATE ON WHAT YOU HAVE READ, THE QUESTIONS YOU HAVE ANSWERED, AND THE STEPS YOU HAVE TAKEN BEFORE PROCEEDING TO THE NEXT CHAPTER OF THIS BOOK.

Chapter 18
ASKING GOD TO STRENGTHEN YOUR FAITH

Are you weak in faith? Do you feel like you just can't make it? Do you feel like you don't know how to get from here to there in life. Do you feel like you don't even know where "there" is? Understand, God wants us to be strong in Him. He wants us to believe that He can and will do whatever needs to be done even when we can't see how it's going to get done. Faith is trusting God even at your weakest moments. It is trusting God even when you don't have all the answers. It's trusting God!

If we take a moment and think about how Jesus taught the disciples through parables and principles the character traits of someone who is following after God and seeking Kingdom living, we see that there was a point where the disciples recognized that they were weak in some areas and asked Jesus to increase their faith. There may be points in time when we see just how frail and weak we are when it comes to trusting, believing, and walking out the Word of God in our lives. It is at that point that we have to remember what Jesus' response was to the disciples. He told them if they had faith as a grain of mustard seed they could say to a sycamine tree to be plucked up by the root and be planted in the sea and it would obey. So if mustard seed faith can move a tree, understand, it can move the mountains of doubt, insecurity, and fear that are rooted in your heart and mind and it can speak and bring forth whatsoever you shall say that is in alignment with God's Word and His will for your life. Understand, it only takes mustard seed faith to shatter the glass of fear so that you can fully walk in faith.

Increasing our faith is not what is necessary in life. What we need to do is to activate the faith that we have. When you activate something, you turn it on and you put it into operation. Too many people are walking around with inactive or dormant faith. If your faith is inoperative, that is like saying you are failing to trust and believe that God can and will do what He has said. Faith in God brings forth the promises of God and we have to walk boldly in our faith in order for the promises to come to pass in our lives.

AS WE BEGIN TO SHATTER THE GLASS OF FEAR, <u>WE MUST UNDERSTAND</u> THAT ...

Faith in God can move mountains. There are many symbolic meanings for mountains in the Bible but in this instance we will look at mountains as a test or trial. So we must understand, if we have faith in God, we can speak to the mountains that rise up in our lives that cause us to walk in fear and cause them to be removed.

> *Mark 11:22-24*
> *And Jesus answering saith unto them, Have faith in God. For verily I say unto you, That whosoever shall say unto this mountain, Be thou removed, and be thou cast into the sea; and shall not doubt in his heart, but shall believe that those things which he saith shall come to pass; he shall have whatsoever he saith. Therefore I say unto you, What things soever ye desire, when ye pray, believe that ye receive them, and ye shall have them.*

* If we are weak in faith and having a hard time trusting and believing that what we need will come to pass, we need to ask God to help our unbelief.

> *Mark 9:23-24*
> *Jesus said unto him, If thou canst believe, all things are possible to him that believeth. And straightway the father of the child cried out, and said with tears, Lord, I believe; help thou mine unbelief.*

AS YOU SHATTER THE GLASS OF FEAR IN YOUR LIFE, <u>ASK YOURSELF</u> ...

Are you having a hard time trusting and believing that God will make a way? Have you asked God to help your unbelief?

ACTION STEP: Take a moment to speak the Word of God over the stressful situations occurring in your life today. Speak to the root of the problem and command a change to take place. Make sure you have scripture that backs up what you are saying. Write down your "go to" scripture for when you are feeling overwhelmed by stress.

> *Isaiah 55:11*
> *So shall my word be that goeth forth out of my mouth: it shall not return unto me void, but it shall accomplish that which I please, and it shall prosper [in the thing] whereto I sent it*

Whether you write it here, in a journal, or on another piece of paper, take time to write down the answers.

1) What is your "go to" scripture when you are feeling overwhelmed by stress?

   _____
   _____
   _____
   _____

2) Why is this your "go to" scripture? What words in this scripture help you build your faith and confidence in God?

   _____
   _____
   _____
   _____

CONFESSION

Father thank you for mountain moving faith. Thank You for the kind of faith that shatters the glass of fear. Today Father, I speak life to every situation concerning my life. I speak peace where there has been turmoil because You said that You would give me the peace that surpasses all of my understanding. I speak increase to the areas of lack in my life because You said that You know the things I have need of and You are faithful and just to provide me with those things. I speak healing to my body because I know that Jesus took stripes on His back for my healing and therefore I am the healed of the Lord and I am saying so. Today I call for my life to come into alignment with Your Word and Your will. If there be any area of my life where I am walking in doubt and unbelief, I ask that You, Father, help my unbelief in Jesus name ... amen.

STOP
TAKE TIME TO MEDITATE ON WHAT YOU HAVE READ, THE QUESTIONS YOU HAVE ANSWERED, AND THE STEPS YOU HAVE TAKEN BEFORE PROCEEDING TO THE NEXT CHAPTER OF THIS BOOK.

Chapter 19
CONFESSING GOD'S WORD IN FAITH

Throughout this book we have been confessing God's Word. At the end of each chapter there is a confession written to help solidify God's Word and His promises in our hearts and minds. The Bible says that faith comes by hearing and hearing by the Word of God. So in order to build our faith, we must be in a position where we hear the Word of God. One definition of the word hear means to learn by the ear or by being told. It also means to give or pay attention to something, to gain information, and to receive communication.[5]

As we receive God's Word, we need to confess it in and over our lives. When we make our confessions of faith, we are admitting and acknowledging that God's Word is true. We are declaring and decreeing what we believe to be true in and over our lives. Understand, confessions can be made both ways. We can have confessions of faith and we could

---

[5] Merriam-Webster.com

have confessions of fear. As we confess God's Word in faith, it will help us to shatter the glass of fear.

God wants us to be strong in the Him and the power of His might. He wants us to stand on His Word and to believe that His Word is true. That's the foundation for faith. We have to be strong in God and believe what He has said is true. We also have to know the purpose of repeating God's Word over and over again in our lives. When we repeat words whether it be words coming out of our mouths or our thoughts, they begin to sink into our subconscious mind and at some point they begin to affect our actions and our behaviors. God's Word is meant to build us up and to help us live our lives in a way where our confidence remains in what He can and will do and not in what we feel we can or cannot do on our own.

AS WE BEGIN TO SHATTER THE GLASS OF FEAR, <u>WE MUST UNDERSTAND</u> THAT ...

* Faith comes by hearing and confessing the Word of God. Hearing is what we are listening to that is coming into our Spirit and confessions is what we are speaking that is coming out of our Spirit. We need to stay in a position where we can always hear God speaking and we need to be quick to open up our mouths in order to rebuke the enemy and confess God's Word over our lives.

> *Romans 10:17*
> *So then faith cometh by hearing, and hearing by the word of God.*

✱ We have to take in God's Word but we also have to speak God's Word in and over our lives because it helps us to discern our thoughts and our intentions. What we think may be entirely different from what we say but God is looking at our heart and He knows o ur every intention.

> *Hebrews 4:12*
> *For the word of God [is] quick, and powerful, and sharper than any twoedged sword, piercing even to the dividing asunder of soul and spirit, and of the joints and marrow, and [is] a discerner of the thoughts and intents of the heart.*

✱ The more Word we know, the stronger our defense is when we come up against spiritual attacks. Knowing what God has said gives us confidence when it comes to believing we are victorious. It also gives us confidence as we rebuke the work of the enemy in and over our lives.

> *I Corinthians 15:57*
> *But thanks be to God, which giveth us the victory through our Lord Jesus Christ.*

AS YOU SHATTER THE GLASS OF FEAR IN YOUR LIFE, ASK YOURSELF ...

Are you confessing God's Word throughout the day over your life? Do you realize confessing the Word you know will help build your confidence in what you believe God will do in and through your life?

ACTION STEP: The Bible talks about the power of the tongue. The tongue is a vital organ that is used for chewing, swallowing, as well as, speech. Take the time to write down 3 personal faith confessions and commit to speaking them over your life every day for the next 30 days. They can be as simple as "I am healed. I am delivered. I am set free."

> *Proverbs 18:21*
> *Death and life are in the power of the tongue, And those who love it will eat its fruit.*

Whether you write it here, in a journal, or on another piece of paper, take time to write down the answers .

1) _____
   _____
   _____
   _____

2) _____
   _____
   _____
   _____

3) _____
   _____
   _____
   _____

CONFESSION

Today is a new day and I am strong in the Lord and the power of His might. Today I speak life to my life. I declare and decree today that I am the healed of the Lord and today all of my needs are met because God said that He would supply all of my needs according to His riches in glory. Today I speak the Word of God over my life and I expect what God has promised to come to pass in my life. Today I know that I am the head and not the tail. I am above only and not beneath. I am victorious because my victory was won at the cross. Today, I declare and I decree that I am free from the yoke of sin and bondage and I am shattering the glass of fear. The bondage of fear that has held me captive in life will no longer have power over my life in Jesus name ... amen.

STOP

TAKE TIME TO MEDITATE ON WHAT YOU HAVE READ, THE QUESTIONS YOU HAVE ANSWERED, AND THE STEPS YOU HAVE TAKEN BEFORE PROCEEDING TO THE NEXT CHAPTER OF THIS BOOK.

Chapter 20
BUILDING ON YOUR FOUNDATION OF FAITH

So you already have faith. You believe God's Word is true. What do you do next? If you trust God, believe God, and you are willing to wait on God, what do you do while you wait? What you have to understand first of all is your faith is going to be challenged. The enemy is not going to sit by idle waiting on you to receive what you say you are believing God for. He is going to try to get you off of the track called faith and put you onto the track of fear and doubt. He is going to try to put you back behind the glass of fear so that you won't be able to fully walk in faith. So what is it that you are going to do to strengthen your stand and stamina in God while you are waiting on Him to perform His promises in your life? It's like being a tree in the midst of a hurricane. While you are standing alone will you be rooted and grounded in the Word and continue to stand in the presence and on the promises of God without wavering?

Do you know what it means to stand? When you stand you have to maintain an upright position. You are settled and you are situated in a particular position. In other words you are set and established. Understand, God wants you to be firm, secure, growing, and flourishing in faith. He doesn't want you fluctuating between faith and fear where you believe Him sometimes and doubt Him at other times. God wants you to come to Him in faith, ask of Him in faith, wait on Him in faith, and to receive His promises by faith.

AS WE BEGIN TO SHATTER THE GLASS OF FEAR, WE MUST UNDERSTAND THAT ...

* The attributes of growing faith include patience and joy. As you continue to grow in faith, you become more patient. Instead of being in fear, you begin to rejoice knowing that God is with you and He has promised to take care of you.

> *James 1:3*
> *Knowing this, that the trying of your faith worketh patience.*

> *I Peter 1:8-9*
> *Whom having not seen, ye love; in whom, though now ye see Him not, yet believing, ye rejoice with joy unspeakable and full of glory: Receiving the end of your faith, even the salvation of your souls.*

�֍ Praying in the Holy Ghost helps you to build up and strengthen your faith. It is the job of the Holy Ghost to build you up in faith. When you pray in the Spirit you strengthen your inner man. Praying in the Spirit also helps you when you don't know what to pray. So understand the Holy Ghost will help us intercede because God knows all things and when we allow His Spirit to lead us in prayer we will pray all things according to His will.

> *Jude 20*
> *But ye, beloved, building up yourselves on your most holy faith, praying in the Holy Ghost,*

�֍ Keeping God and His Word at the forefront of everything you say and do will help you grow strong in faith because God's Word will bring with it life, health, and strength.

> *Proverbs 4:20-22*
> *My son, attend to my words; incline thine ear unto my sayings. Let them not depart from thine eyes; keep them in the midst of thine heart. For they are life unto those that find them, and health to all their flesh.*

AS YOU SHATTER THE GLASS OF FEAR IN YOUR LIFE, <u>ASK YOURSELF</u> ...

Are you rooted and grounded in faith? Do you feel the Word you know will be able to sustain you when you come against the rough winds that come with life?

ACTION STEP: Look up 10 scriptures that talk about being and staying in faith. Write them down and read them every day for the 7 days. Let those scriptures help strengthen your foundation. On day 8, find 10 different scriptures on faith. Write them down and read them for the next 7 days and do the same on day 15. Read over and confess the scriptures you write down about faith for 21 days and let it help strengthen and grow your foundation of faith.

Matthew 4:4
But he answered and said, It is written, Man shall not live by bread alone, but by every word that proceedeth out of the mouth of God.

Whether you write it here, in a journal, or on another piece of paper, take time to write down the answers .

1) _____
   _____
   _____
   _____

2) _____
_____
_____
_____

3) _____
_____
_____
_____

4) _____
_____
_____
_____

5) _____
_____
_____
_____

6) _____
_____
_____
_____

7) _____
_____
_____
_____

8) _____
_____
_____
_____

9) _____
_____
_____
_____

10) _____
_____
_____
_____

DAY 8, WRITE DOWN 10 MORE SCRIPTURES ABOUT FAITH

1) _____
_____
_____
_____

2) _____
_____
_____
_____

3) _____
_____
_____
_____

4) _____
   _____
   _____
   _____

5) _____
   _____
   _____
   _____

6) _____
   _____
   _____
   _____

7) _____
   _____
   _____
   _____

8) _____
   _____
   _____
   _____

9) _____
   _____
   _____
   _____

10) _____
_____
_____
_____

DAY 15, WRITE DOWN 10 MORE SCRIPTURES ABOUT FAITH

1) _____
_____
_____
_____

2) _____
_____
_____
_____

3) _____
_____
_____
_____

4) _____
_____
_____
_____

5) _____
_____
_____
_____

6) _____
_____
_____
_____

7) _____
_____
_____
_____

8) _____
_____
_____
_____

9) _____
_____
_____
_____

10) _____
_____
_____
_____

CONFESSION

Father today I am standing and staying on Your Word. I am speaking faith filled words because I know that You are faithful. Father I am strong in You. I am whole in You. I have all that I need because I know that You are my supplier so as long as I have You there is nothing lacking in my life. Father, I am healed. I am delivered. I am more than a conqueror in You. Today I will walk in faith, stand in faith, wait in faith, and receive the promises of my faith in Jesus name ... amen.

STOP

TAKE TIME TO MEDITATE ON WHAT YOU HAVE READ, THE QUESTIONS YOU HAVE ANSWERED, AND THE STEPS YOU HAVE TAKEN BEFORE PROCEEDING TO THE NEXT CHAPTER OF THIS BOOK.

Chapter 21
CONTINUING IN FAITH

Fear and doubt will come to challenge your faith but the question is, will you continue to walk in faith when fear and doubt comes? We have to remember that faith if believing and trusting in what God said He would do. It is having your total reliance on God and not on self.

Faith is not automatic but is something we must have and there are things we must do in order to stay in faith. We can have weak faith or we can do what is necessary in order for our faith to grow and to be strong. Before we can truly walk in faith we have to fully believe God. It's not about believing God can do some things in our lives. It's about believing He can do all things in our lives.

When we think about what it means to continue, we think about carrying on or resuming what has been interrupted. Challenges come to interrupt your faith but you have to remain steadfast and immovable and you have to continue to believe and trust that God will do what He said He would do. Even if the glass of fear comes back up in your life, you have remember that it is a hindrance and hindrances can be removed. You have to remember that all it takes is faith to shatter the glass of fear.

AS WE BEGIN TO SHATTER THE GLASS OF FEAR, <u>WE MUST UNDERSTAND</u> THAT …

✳ Living by faith is not automatic. The Bible talks about the just living by faith. Remember, faith is a lifestyle. It is the way you style your life. Evil people are not going to live their lives by having faith in God but those who are just or should I say those who are conforming to God's truth, shall live by faith.

> *Hebrews 10:38*
> *Now the just shall live by faith: but if any man draw back, my soul shall have no pleasure in him.*

✳ We can choose to walk by faith or we can choose to walk according to what we see but we have to remember, living by what we see can facilitate and perpetuate fear in our lives and God wants us living by faith, NOT fear. We have to learn how to see life through our spiritual eyes of faith.

> *2 Corinthians 5:7*
> *For we walk by faith, not by sight:*

AS YOU SHATTER THE GLASS OF FEAR IN YOUR LIFE, ASK YOURSELF ...

Are you letting what you see dictate what you do or are you letting what God said dictate what you do? Faith requires us to trust God in-spite of what we see.

ACTION STEP: Write down 3 things in your life that you see are going contrary to what God said and speak God's Word over them. If you see lack, speak that God will supply your needs according His riches in glory. If you see sickness and disease, speak that you are healed by the stripes of Jesus. Whatever it is that is contrary to God's Word, speak the Word to it and command it to change in Jesus name.

> *Matthew 4:4*
> *But he answered, "It is written, "'Man shall not live by bread alone, but by every word that comes from the mouth of God."*

Whether you write it here, in a journal, or on another piece of paper, take time to write down the answers.

1) _____
   _____
   _____
   _____

2) _____
   _____
   _____
   _____

3) _____
   _____
   _____
   _____

CONFESSION

Father today I speak words of faith. I speak that I am the healed of You. I speak that every one of my needs are met. I speak that I am covered and kept by the blood of Jesus. I speak today that I have right and righteous thoughts. Today I speak to myself and command my "self", the part of me that is different from everyone else, to be in alignment with who and what You are. I command my characteristics to mimic Yours and I command my thoughts to be conducive to yours in Jesus name ... amen.

STOP

TAKE TIME TO MEDITATE ON WHAT YOU HAVE READ, THE QUESTIONS YOU HAVE ANSWERED, AND THE STEPS YOU HAVE TAKEN BEFORE PROCEEDING TO THE NEXT CHAPTER OF THIS BOOK.

Chapter 22
YIELDING THE FRUIT OF YOUR FAITH

After you have shattered the glass of fear and you are walking fully in faith, what kind of crop are you getting when you walk in faith? Are you yielding the fruit of your faith? To yield means to bear and to bring forth. It means to produce or furnish as a return on investment.[6] Understand, walking in faith is our investment and we should be bearing the fruit of God's Word in our lives.

Remember, fruit comes from a seed. The seed has to be planted in order for fruit to come from it. Yielding the fruit of our faith is a result of the seed which is the Word of God being planted in our hearts and minds. The fruit that comes forth in our lives comes in the form of love, joy, peace, patience, kindness, goodness, faithfulness, gentleness, and self-control. It also comes in the form of

---
[6] Merriam-Webster Online

blessings where we begin to see God's Word operative in our lives and those things which we hope and pray for begin to break forth into the physical realm as we continue to walk in faith believing that nothing is impossible for God.

Just as fruit is good for our physical body, it is also good for the nourishment of our soul to bear Kingdom fruit. Bearing the fruit of our faith solidifies our testimonies and it allows others to see the faithfulness of God.

AS WE BEGIN TO SHATTER THE GLASS OF FEAR, WE MUST UNDERSTAND THAT ...

* Your heart is the ground (the earth) in which God is planting His Word and God wants that Word to multiply and grow within you.

> *Genesis 1:11*
> *And God said, Let the earth bring forth grass, the herb yielding seed, and the fruit tree yielding fruit after his kind, whose seed is in itself, upon the earth: and it was so.*

* We must understand that the Word of God is like a seed and the seed of God's Word is sown into our heart. However, the ground on which it is sown matters. If the ground of our heart is not right, the Word sown will not take root.

> *Matthew 1:3-9*
> *And he spake many things unto them in parables, saying, Behold, a sower went forth to sow; And when he sowed, some seeds fell by the way side, and the fowls came and devoured them up: Some fell upon stony places, where they had not much earth: and forthwith they sprung up, because they had no deepness of earth: And when the sun was up, they were scorched; and because they had no root, they withered away. And some fell among thorns; and the thorns sprung up, and choked them: But other fell into good ground, and brought forth fruit, some an hundredfold, some sixtyfold, some thirtyfold. Who hath ears to hear, let him hear.*

AS YOU SHATTER THE GLASS OF FEAR IN YOUR LIFE, ASK YOURSELF ...

Have you tilled the ground of your heart to prepare it to receive the Word of God? Is your heart open and ready for the Word to take root? Are there stones of bitterness, anger, and strife still in the ground of your heart waiting to hinder and to keep the fruit of God's Word from growing?

ACTION STEP: Pluck up the stones. The stones would be anything that you know is still in your heart that can hinder God's Word and faith from growing and bringing forth fruit. Pluck up the stones of bitterness and unforgiveness and whatever else you know will hinder you from receiving the blessings of God. Write down anything you may be harboring in your heart that you know goes against the will and the Word of God. Bind it up, cast it out, and pray that it will no longer be able to take root in your heart and mind.

> *Matthew 13:20*
> *But he that received the seed into stony places, the same is he that heareth the word, and anon with joy receiveth it;*

Whether you write it here, in a journal, or on another piece of paper, take time to write down your answers.

_____
_____
_____
_____
_____
_____
_____
_____
_____
_____
_____
_____

CONFESSION

Father today I prepare my heart to receive Your Word. Your Word is true. I believe Your Word and I believe that Your Word works. As I receive Your Word in my heart, I believe my faith will increase and I shall see the fruit of my faith. Today I speak forth multiplied blessings in my life that will include the fruit of Your Spirit. Today I will walk in love, joy, peace, patience, kindness, goodness, faithfulness, gentleness, and self-control as I wait on You to manifest Your abundant blessings in my life according to my faith in You in Jesus name ... amen.

STOP

TAKE TIME TO MEDITATE ON WHAT YOU HAVE READ, THE QUESTIONS YOU HAVE ANSWERED, AND THE STEPS YOU HAVE TAKEN BEFORE PROCEEDING TO THE NEXT CHAPTER OF THIS BOOK.

Chapter 23
FINISHING FAITH

So let's talk about finishing faith. The faith that says you believe God will finish what He has started. Fearless faith because the glass of fear is now gone. The faith that comes and the faith that stays. The Bible says that He who began a good work in you is faithful to complete it. You have to settle it in your heart and mind that God is able to finish what He has started. No matter what tricks, traps and roadblocks the enemy brings your way, you have to believe that God will do it. He will finish what He started. When you walk in finishing faith, the glass of fear is shattered, and you believe that He who began a good work in you is faithful to complete it.

Let's think about the word finish. The last words that Jesus spoke on the cross was "it is finished". To finish means to accomplish, to complete, and to bring through to the end. Jesus accomplished what He came to the earth to do. He fulfilled the Word that had already been spoken. We have to understand that God will also fulfill the words that He has spoken in and over our lives. We have to believe God to the end so that we can see the reality of His promises come forth in our lives.

Finishing faith is faith in God's Word that has been fulfilled. When something is fulfilled, the expectation is met and the standard is complete.   You can fill a glass half full and have some of what you need to quench your thirst but understand, God wants your life to be full to the overflow. He wants you to experience His best for your life and He wants you to trust Him to do what He said He would do. As it says in 2 Timothy, we need to fight the good fight of faith, to finish the course, and to keep the faith so that we can receive the crown of righteousness that has been laid up for us.

AS WE FINISH SHATTERING THE GLASS OF FEAR, WE MUST UNDERSTAND THAT ...

✳ Finishing faith brings with it a crown of righteousness.

> *2 Timothy 4:7-8*
> *I have fought a good fight, I have finished my course, I have kept the faith: Henceforth there is laid up for me a crown of righteousness, which the Lord, the righteous judge, shall give me at that day: and not to me only, but unto all them also that love his appearing.*

* You have to remain confident and believe that God will finish what He has started in your life.   Faith comes from God and our faith must remain in God.

> *Philippians 1:6*
> *For I am confident of this very thing, that He who began a good work in you will perfect it until the day of Christ Jesus.*

* Just as God gave Solomon an assignment and he finished it.   We too must finish the assignment God has given us to do.   We must be a light in the midst of darkness and we must trust God to complete His good work in us.

> *I Kings 6:14*
> *So Solomon built the house and finished it.*

AS YOU SHATTER THE GLASS OF FEAR IN YOUR LIFE, ASK YOURSELF ...

Do you have confidence in the fact that God can finish the good work that He has started in you?   Are you ready to finish the course?   Understanding that the course is the route or direction God has given you to follow. It is the race in which we have already been empowered to win.

ACTION STEP: Write down 5 things that God has placed in your heart to do that are in alignment with His Word, His will, and His way. Now pray that He gives you the course or should I say directions that He wants you to follow in order to get these things done. Make sure you commit to following the course He gives you while staying in faith.

Habakkuk 2:2-3
And the Lord answered me, and said, Write the vision, and make it plain upon tables, that he may run that readeth it. For the vision is yet for an appointed time, but at the end it shall speak, and not lie: though it tarry, wait for it; because it will surely come, it will not tarry.

Whether you write it here, in a journal, or on another piece of paper, take time to write down the answers .

1) _____
_____
_____
_____

2) _____
_____
_____
_____

3) _____
_____

4) _____

_____

_____

_____

5) _____

_____

_____

_____

CONFESSION

Father today I break through the glass of fear and I commit to walking fully in faith. I will not look to the right nor to the left. I will keep my eyes stayed on You. My hope and my expectation are both in You. I know that You began this good work in me and You are faithful to complete it. I trust You to do just that. Finish in me the good work that You have began. I believe Your Word is true and I believe You are Alpha and Omega, the beginning and the end. So I know that You will do what You said because there is no incompletion in You. You finish what You start in Jesus name ... amen.

STOP

TAKE TIME TO MEDITATE ON WHAT YOU HAVE READ, THE QUESTIONS YOU HAVE ANSWERED, AND THE STEPS YOU HAVE TAKEN BEFORE PROCEEDING TO THE NEXT CHAPTER OF THIS BOOK.

Chapter 24
TALKING ABOUT SCRIPTURE AS IT RELATES TO YOUR FAITH

There are many scriptures in the Bible that talk about faith and being faithful. Here are just a few for your to meditate on. God wants us to stay in faith and He also wants us to prove ourselves as faithful. Faith says you believe and trust God. Being faithful says that God can believe and trust you.

☑ WHAT DOUBT WILL DO TO YOUR FAITH

When doubt enters in, it cancels out our faith. We can't say we believe God and doubt God at the same time. Belief awaits the promise, whereas, doubt cancels out our faith. When we doubt, we are saying that we don't fully believe in what God can and will do for us.

SCRIPTURE MEDITATION

Matthew 14:31 - And immediately Jesus stretched forth [his] hand, and caught him, and said unto him, O thou of little faith, wherefore didst thou doubt?

☑ HAVING LITTLE OR NO FAITH

God wants us to trust Him, believe Him and to wait on Him. He said that He will hide His face from those who are difficult, contrary, and have no faith. We must understand, faith is a requirement.

One of the things we need to do is to look at what God has done to help fuel our faith to help us believe what He will do what we need Him to do it. He wants us to look at and see how He dresses and clothes the grass of the field so that we can trust, believe, and know that He will do the same for us.

Having little faith causes us to walk in fear. Little faith doesn't really take God at His Word and when storms arise in our lives, we don't have the faith we need to rebuke the storms and to believe that God will shield us, protect us, and keep us no matter what is going on around us.

SCRIPTURE MEDITATION
Deuteronomy 32:20 - And he said, I will hide my face from them, I will see what their end [shall be]: for they [are] a very froward generation, children in whom [is] no faith.

Matthew 6:30 - Wherefore, if God so clothe the grass of the field, which to day is, and tomorrow is cast into the oven, [shall he] not much more [clothe] you, O ye of little faith?

Matthew 8:26 - And he saith unto them, Why are ye fearful, O ye of little faith? Then he arose, and rebuked the winds and the sea; and there was a great calm.

☑ LIVING BY FAITH

We have to live by faith. As we think about a just person living by faith, we think about a person who is in right standing with God. They are thinking, speaking, seeking, and relying on God for whatever they have need of in life. Living by faith says that our hope and our trust are both in God.

Faith is not limited to a specific timeframe. Faith is a walk that we must take every moment of every day until Jesus returns. The Bible specifically asks the question about whether or not Jesus will find faith in the earth whenever He returns. So walking in faith is not a momentary action, it is a consistent life-long action. It is a lifestyle. It is a day-by-day walk that we have to take with God. It is a reminder of how Adam walked with God prior to sin and self-reliance coming into the earth. That is how we need to walk with God in faith.

SCRIPTURE MEDITATION
Habakkuk 2:4 - Behold, his soul [which] is lifted up is not upright in him: but the just shall live by his faith.

Luke 18:8 - I tell you that he will avenge them speedily. Nevertheless when the Son of man cometh, shall he find faith on the earth?

☑ FAITH WILL BRING WITH IT HEALING AND WHOLENESS

Before we can walk in faith, our knowledge of God should lead us to a place where our trust is completely in Him. Trusting God means we believe what He has said. One of the ways that God describes Himself in the Word is as the Healer and we have to believe that He will take sickness and disease from the midst of us. We have to believe that with God comes not only healing but wholeness. When you are whole, there is nothing lacking, missing, or broken.

SCRIPTURE MEDITATION

Matthew 9:22 - But Jesus turned him about, and when he saw her, he said, Daughter, be of good comfort; thy faith hath made thee whole. And the woman was made whole from that hour.

Matthew 15:28 - Then Jesus answered and said unto her, O woman, great [is] thy faith: be it unto thee even as thou wilt. And her daughter was made whole from that very hour.

Mark 10:52 - And Jesus said unto him, Go thy way; thy faith hath made thee whole. And immediately he received his sight, and followed Jesus in the way.

Luke 7:50 - And He said to the woman, Thy faith hath saved thee; go in peace.

Luke 17:19 - And he said unto him, Arise, go thy way: thy faith hath made thee whole.

Mark 5:34 - And he said unto her, Daughter, thy faith hath made thee whole; go in peace, and be whole of thy plague.

Matthew 9:29 - Then touched he their eyes, saying, According to your faith be it unto you.

☑ FAITH BRINGS WITH IT FORGIVENESS

Living by faith also brings with it forgiveness. When Jesus saw the faith of the people who brought forth the man sick of palsy lying on his bed, not only did He heal the man, He said unto the man that his sins had been forgiven and then He told him to take up his bed and walk. Walking fully in faith also opens the door for us to walk in the forgiveness of God that we have been given.

SCRIPTURE MEDITATION

Matthew 9:2 - And, behold, they brought to him a man sick of the palsy, lying on a bed: and Jesus seeing their faith said unto the sick of the palsy; Son, be of good cheer; thy sins be forgiven thee.

Luke 5:20 - And when he saw their faith, he said unto him, Man, thy sins are forgiven thee.

☑ FAITH THAT OVERRIDES FEAR

Our faith is meant to override our fear. We can either walk in faith or we can dwell in fear. Walking in faith says that we trust and believe that God will do what He said He would do but dwelling in fear says that we are afraid to move and afraid to trust in what God said He could and would do through His Word. Fear says we are afraid of what will happen next. It says that we don't fully trust God to take care of us. God wants us to walk in faith and He wants us to cast down all fear. So if fear arises in our hearts and mind, we have to bind it up and cast it down. We have to trust God and take God at His Word.

SCRIPTURE MEDITATION
Mark 4:40 - And he said unto them, Why are ye so fearful? how is it that ye have no faith?

Luke 8:25 - And he said unto them, Where is your faith? And they being afraid wondered, saying one to another, What manner of man is this! for he commandeth even the winds and water, and they obey him.

☑ GREAT FAITH

Great faith is faith that will help us believe for the impossible. When we believe in God, we have to settle it within our heart and mind that with God, all things are possible. God is the Creator of heaven and earth. He created man and breathed life into him. Nothing could be made or done without the power of God. It is only God that makes life possible.

SCRIPTURE MEDITATION
Matthew 8:10 - When Jesus heard [it], he marvelled, and said to them that followed, Verily I say unto you, I have not found so great faith, no, not in Israel.

Matthew 17:20 - And Jesus said unto them, Because of your unbelief: for verily I say unto you, If ye have faith as a grain of mustard seed, ye shall say unto this mountain, Remove hence to yonder place; and it shall remove; and nothing shall be impossible unto you.

☑ THE OBJECT OF YOUR FAITH

Faith has a focus and God has to be the object of our faith. He has the be the focal point. When you focus in on something, it becomes your center of attention and God needs to always be the center of our attention. We have to keep our eyes, our minds, and our hearts stayed on Him. It is easy to become distracted in life but we have to remember that it is only God that can help us make it in life.

SCRIPTURE MEDITATION
Mark 11:22 - And Jesus answering saith unto them, Have faith in God.

☑ FAITH HELPS YOU TO SEE
Faith gives you the ability to see. When we walk in faith, we choose to see life and the situations in life through the lens of God's Word and His love We see as God sees and we know that all things are possible in and through Christ. Fear blinds us. Fear keeps us from being able to see and comprehend the promises of God. It overshadows faith and it locks up our thoughts and emotions to the point that we are not able to even comprehend how to walk in faith. Think about when you are afraid, the biggest cry of our heart is "Lord, what am I going to do".

SCRIPTURE MEDITATION
Acts 26:18 - To open their eyes, [and] to turn [them] from darkness to light, and [from] the power of Satan unto God, that they may receive forgiveness of sins, and inheritance among them which are sanctified by faith that is in me.

☑ UNFAILING FAITH
Unfailing faith is faith that will not fail under pressure. It is the faith that stands the test of time and after you have been through, you help bring others through. We have to understand what it means to fail before we can understand what it means to have unfailing faith. To fail means that something is lacking or deficient. It means to be unsuccessful. We have to remember that God's Holy Spirit resides on the inside of us and there is nothing lacking or insufficient in us. We have to also remember that the Bible tells us that we can do all things through Christ which

strengthens us. The knowledge of God being in us and with us has to the be the foundation of our faith. Knowing that we are not alone should empower us to stand and stay in faith so that our faith fails not.

SCRIPTURE MEDITATION
I Peter 1:7 - That the trial of your faith, being much more precious than of gold that perisheth, though it be tried with fire, might be found unto praise and honour and glory at the appearing of Jesus Christ:

Luke 22:32 - But I have prayed for thee, that thy faith fail not: and when thou art converted, strengthen thy brethren.

☑ MIRACLE WORKING FAITH

Miracle working faith believes that God can do whatever needs to be done. No matter how bleak the situation may be, miracle working faith has to believe that God can do all things and it must believe that nothing is too hard for God. In the Bible we see where God worked miracles all the time, we have to settle it within our heart and minds that the miracles that God did in the Old and New Testament are still being done today. People are still being healed and breakthroughs are still coming forth. God has not changed. The only thing that has changed in the earth is how the people in the earth view God and how the atmosphere of faith has changed. In the Bible, the people had cohesive faith. They were committed, they were dedicated, and they believed in unison. We have to remember there is power in unity and a unified atmosphere of faith sets the atmosphere for God to move in supernatural ways.

SCRIPTURE MEDITATION
Acts 6:8 - And Stephen, full of faith and power, did great wonders and miracles among the people.

Acts 14:9 - The same heard Paul speak: who steadfastly beholding him, and perceiving that he had faith to be healed,

ABOUT THE AUTHOR

R. Lynn Moore is the Author of an online Facebook Blog called Daily Moments With God (www.Facebook.com/DailyMomentsWithGodWithRLynnMoore). She is the mother of two and the grandmother of three. Her journey with God begin 30 years ago when she moved to a new state as a single mother where she only knew one person and at that time she had to learn how to totally rely on God. Her journey with God has not been an easy one. There have been many tests, trials, and struggles along the way but she has learned over the years how important it is to let your faith override your fears and it is that faith in God that has led her to write this book in an effort to help others overcome the challenges that come against their faith that they are encountering in life. Her desire is to help others learn how to push past their doubt and fears to the point that they trust God completely. Understanding when something is complete, it has all the components necessary to do whatever needs to be done.

Made in the USA
Monee, IL
02 October 2023